MW00352842

The Treatises

of

A COURSE OF

LOVE

THE COURSE OF LOVE SERIES

The Treatises

of

A COURSE OF

LOVE

COURSE OF LOVE PUBLICATIONS
ST. PAUL, MINNESOTA

Course of Love Publications
432 Rehnberg Place
W. St. Paul, Minnesota 55118
www.acourseoflove.com
acol@thedialogues.com

Copyright 2001 by Mari Perron.
All rights reserved.

First Course of Love Publications Edition
Printed in the United States of America

ISBN 0-9728668-3-3
ISBN 13: 978-0-9728668-3-5

This edition is printed on 60 lb. Vellum natural recycled paper.

Distributed in the United States by Itasca Books
Prism Publishing Center
5120 Cedar Lake Road
Minneapolis, MN 55416
www.ItascaBooks.com

A Treatise on the
ART OF THOUGHT

A Treatise on the
NATURE OF UNITY AND ITS RECOGNITION

A Treatise on the
PERSONAL SELF

A Treatise on the
NEW

CONTENTS

FOREWORD

A year or so after the Course of Love series was complete, "Learning in the Time of Christ" was provided as an aid to those questioning how to work with the material of this Course. It has been edited here to serve as an introduction to the Treatises. The full text is available from the Course of Love website: www.acourseoflove.com.

The Treatises bring the same situation you encountered in receiving the Course of Love, but you will now encounter these situations in life. You are no longer only a reader. Your experience of this Course has extended beyond reading and beyond the classroom situation. Now a time may come when studying truly seems to be in order. The guidance provided by your reading may seem to come and go and your desire to rely on what you have "learned" will grow. You may desire to backtrack, review, or begin to highlight passages to return to again and again. New questions may arise and a desire for feedback or discussion grow stronger. This may also be precisely the time when you are so caught up in experience and learning "in life" that return to a group or classroom situation feels next to impossible.

Now you are experiencing life in a new way and will be attempting to reinforce what you already know and have already accepted. The "language" is returned to as a helpful friend would be turned to for judgment-free advice. What those who begin to experience life in a new way begin to discover are the patterns of thoughts and behavior that are most deeply entrenched. You feel in need of assistance!

You may need to become more flexible, meet in groups less frequently, and favor more casual and spontaneous encounters. Yet what is being gained through experience is still in need of being shared. This sharing can offer a rich and rewarding opportunity for differences to be revealed and for the welcome realization that differences do not make separate.

The forward motion is one away from learning and toward acceptance of what is. While differences may be highlighted in this time, what will be revealed through sharing is that while experiences may differ greatly and seem to be offering diverse "learning" situations, you, and those with whom you share, will actually be coming to many very similar new insights and truths.

The impatience of the earlier level may seem to have increased as your experiences will be moving you along at your own pace. Comparisons may arise and some may feel they are not advancing as quickly as others, while those moving quickly may feel in need of time to catch their breath!

Inclinations may be strong during this time, to "figure things out." Problem solving is discouraged. Trust is encouraged. Question: "How might I be able to look at a situation in a new way?" Remembering the gentleness of the Art of Thought over the relentless stridency of the thinking mind is helpful. Obsessive thinking is always ruthless, judgmental, and wearing on you.

The entrenched patterns of the past are difficult to dislodge even when they have been recognized. "Watch the parade go by" as what has gone unhealed is brought forward for acceptance, forgiveness, and letting go. With the letting go of each old pattern or situation that seems fraught with peril, a cloud of despair will lift, a little more of darkness recede, and a little more light be available to show the way.

xiv

Here you may meet individual assessment and self-doubt. You may wonder if you are missing something. You may feel as if you have not experienced unity or as if you are no closer to knowing yourself or God. You may feel as if this course of study that seemed to be working so well for a while, now is letting you down. You may wonder where and when the peace, ease, and abundance promised by this course will arrive. Stay grounded in the present and remember that you are no longer seeking. This time of engagement with life is just what is needed to integrate what has been learned. A return to the simple words that begin the Treatise on Unity would be appropriate: "A treasure that you do not as yet recognize is going to be recognized. Once recognized it will begin to be regarded as an ability. And finally, through experience it will become your identity."

The achievements of the past, achievements that awarded credentials, certificates, and degrees, admiration, respect, and status, are now a thing of the past. What you may well be looking for is your reward for the investment you have made in this coursework. While you are looking for it to show up in an old way you will miss the new ways that are being revealed. The achievements of the past were not lasting and they are not what you would truly want now. The goal is reached in being who you are at last. It is present—not in the future. It is with you—not beyond you. The treasure is you.

A Treatise on the ART OF THOUGHT

The First Treatise

chapter 1

the First Instruction

1.1 A split mind does not learn for a split mind is incapable of giving and receiving as one. A split mind does not rest for it can find no peace. A state of peace is a prerequisite of giving and receiving as one. Any state other than that of peace is conflicted by the desire for peace and the ways in which peace is seen as being approachable. Peace is seen as being outside of one's being and the means are sought for the union of being with that which will provide for peace. Knowing not what this is, is the source of conflict and of all seeking. No one seeks for what they already know how to find or for what they already believe they possess.

1.2 While *A Course of Love* has led you to a state of wholeness of mind and heart, or wholeheartedness, your realization of this state of being requires further guidance. This treatise will attempt to give specific examples of what to look for as your learning continues, or how to identify wholehearted responses from those of a split mind. Its further purpose is to identify the service that you can provide once your wholeheartedness is completely realized.

1.3 The first instruction I give you is to seek no more. All that you are in need of knowing has been provided within *A Course of Love*. That your learning does not feel complete is not a failing of the Course or of yourself. That your learning does not feel complete is the result of forgetfulness, which is the opposite of mindfulness. Your further learning then is learning based on mindfulness or remembering.

1.4 *A Course of Love* has provided you with what you need to know, which is the function of all course work. This does not mean that you have acquired the ability to live what you have learned, only that you are ready to. The very word "remember," as well as the concept of memory, implies mindfulness and the ability to reproduce or recall both what has been learned and what has been experienced. Reproducing and recollecting are acts of creation. They do not bring back a reality that once was but transform that reality into a present moment experience. It is in the present-moment experience memory provides that truth, rather than illusion, can now be experienced and learned from. It is in the present-moment experience that you will receive the blessing of being able to respond differently to love.

1.5 All that you have experienced in truth is love. All that illusion provided you with was nothing. Your first task as you remember and re-experience is that of separating illusion from the truth. This will require no effort for what you have learned in this Course has prepared you for this task. As each situation that re-enacts a previous learning experience arises, you will, if you trust your heart, be perfectly able to identify illusion from truth. This is a simple act of recognizing meaning. All that you believe you learned from illusion will have no meaning to you now and will allow you to give up any remnants of false learning you acquired. All that you learned in error from identifying love incorrectly will be relearned as love is properly identified.

1.6 Although I have just instructed you to trust in your heart, your reunited mind and heart will now be called to act in unison. That *A Course of Love* instructed you little in the mechanics of the mind was consistent with its theme and learning goals. The mechanics of the mind can, in truth, be left behind as we concentrate rather on the art of thought.

1.7 The mechanics of the mind were what engaged you in so many daily battles that you became almost too weary to continue. The mechanics of the mind were what were in need of being overcome in order for you to listen once again to the wisdom of your heart. The mechanics of your over-worked and over-stimulated mind were what you were asked to leave behind, as this act of leaving behind was the only means by which you could allow your mind to be restful enough for it to even contemplate union or the new learning required to facilitate your return to union. Your return to union is your return to love and it is accessed at the center or heart of your self. Your mind was in need of silencing in order for you to hear the wisdom of your heart and begin your return. Now, in order to complete your return, mind and heart must work as one.

1.8 You are a thinking being. This cannot be denied nor should it be. A course that left you with an erroneous impression that relying on feeling alone would complete your learning would in actuality leave your learning incomplete. Without this Treatise on the Art of Thought, too many of you would become muddled in your feelings and know not where to turn to explain the many riddles they would seem at times to represent.

1.9 A mind and heart joined in union abolishes the ego. The ego-mind was what was once in charge of all your thoughts. Since the ego is incapable of learning, the ego-mind had to be circumvented in order for true learning to take place. This is what *A Course of Love* accomplished. This learning was accomplished in you, making you The Accomplished. As The Accomplished, you now are able to access universal mind.

1.10 The joy that will come to you from the thoughts of a mind joined in union will be unparalleled in your experience here. "Ah," you will say with a relief and joy that knows no bounds, "this is what it is to experience and know the truth.

5

This is what it is to create for this is what it is like to think as God thinks." Where once you recognized only illusion, and called it reality, the mind joined in union will now, more and more, recognize only truth and experience only the truly real.

1.11   You can already imagine what an extensive change this will bring. As you are still experiencing change in time, without guidance, this change would be seen as quite difficult no matter how grand its outcome and even in spite of your recognition, at first in mere fleeting moments, that it is a change you would welcome.

1.12   Again your willingness is called upon. Be willing now to apply the art of thought to the experience of truth.

chapter 2

the Art of Thought

2.1   The closing pages of *A Course of Love* instructed you to think no more.   A break in time was needed for you to disengage the ego-mind that produced the type of thinking that needs to come to an end.   This ending is but a beginning in truth and has led you to readiness to learn the art of thought.

2.2   We identified much for you to leave behind within the pages of *A Course of Love*.   These many things which seemed so distinct and separate and which ranged from fear, to struggle, to effort, to control and protection, can all now be seen as the products of the thoughts of your ego-mind.

2.3   To experience the truth and apply to that experience the thoughts of the ego-mind, the same thoughts that were applied to former experiences of the truth, would be to respond to love the same way again.   The questions you have asked concerning how love could be the answer when it has been preached by so many for so long are answered here.   The answer lies in your response to love.   To respond is to answer.   You have sought your "answer" everywhere, but here is where it lies.   It is yours to give and can only be given to love from love.   Only in giving is it received.

2.4   Thus we have sought to uncover your Source, to provide you access to your heart from which all responses flow.   As your heart is the Source of your true Self, your thoughts, once removed from those of the ego-mind are about the expression and extension of your true Self. They are the answer of the created to the creator, the answer of the Self to God.

2.5   Thoughts that were guarded by the ego-mind were in need of being set free. Appealing to your heart was the means or cause of this freedom being accomplished in you. What was spoken of within *A Course of Love* as unlearning has begun and continues here. What was spoken of within *A Course of Love* as new learning has begun and continues here as well. The difference is that you are now ready to learn a new means of response to this unlearning and learning. That response is the art of thought.

2.6   The so-called thinking of the ego-mind was so tyrannical that its use throughout your lifetime deadened many of your feelings. The ego-mind led you so far from the truth that you no longer trust in it. It confused the smallest issues to such a degree that it left you unable to respond purely to anything. The so-called thinking of the ego-mind could be likened to chitchat, background noise, static. So little meaning did it have that all meaning became muddled.

2.7   Your only recourse to this situation in the past was focus. Thus you applied your thoughts to learning subjects of a specific nature. Through this focus you believed you accomplished much. You congratulated yourself on having the discipline required to train your mind to focus and to learn or shamed yourself when you were unable to do so. To those most skilled in this training of the ego-mind worldly rewards have long been given. These people attain degrees and skills and then further apply the discipline that they have learned by using their skills and knowledge in the world for even greater rewards. These rewards have further emphasized the importance of such focused thoughts and further entrenched the ego-mind. To think that you could learn the truth of who you are through these same means was the fallacy that the early teaching of *A Course of Love* sought to dispel.

2.8   But again, as was stated often throughout this Course, an alternative exists. It did not exist when you knew not of it and so your attempts at learning have been valiant and are no cause for anxiety now. But now this alternative is being revealed to you and it does call for a change of thought so extensive that all thought as you once knew it does need to cease.

2.9   You have already succeeded in learning in this new way once or you would not be here. This is your proof that you can do so again and again until the new way totally replaces the old and the art of thought leaves behind forever the need for what the ego-mind once but seemed to offer you.

2.10   The thoughts of your ego-mind were ruled by the nature of the body. To exist as *creatures* whose only thoughts are of survival of the body is to exist in a lower order. The laws of the body have subjected you to conditions that invited the ego-mind to turn its attention to existence in this lower order. It is only *you* who can recognize and invite the higher order or subject *yourself* to its conditions. It is only your attention to the existence of this higher order that will reveal its laws to you. These are the laws of God or the laws of love.

2.11   The laws of God or the laws of love can be summarized by the simple statement of giving and receiving being one in truth. The implications of this statement are far broader than at first might seem indicated. All of these implications have been touched upon within *A Course of Love*. The most essential of these implications is that of relationship, for giving and receiving cannot occur without relationship.

2.12   All relationship is but relationship between creator and created. The new means of thinking is referred to here as the "art" of thought in order to call your wholehearted attention to the continual act of creation that is the relationship between creator and created. Creation is but a dialogue to which you have not responded. The art of thought will free you to respond.

2.13   An example illustrates. To look at a sunset is to see an object: the sun. It is also to see the sky, to see the variety of colors displayed, to see the horizon. It is to see the surrounding area, perhaps to see the play of clouds among the descending rays, or to feel the warmth or chill of an evening. The whole experience might include the sound of birds or traffic, the rhythm of the ocean, or the pounding of your own heart. This sunset might be an experience in which you share the awe inspired by this sight with one you love. It might be seen as you walk or drive, rake leaves, or gaze from an office window. It might be a deathbed vision or the first sunset of which a young child is aware. It might be a scene taken totally for granted as you go about whatever business calls you at that hour. This response needs to at first be seen in two parts.

2.14   The sunset is a gift of God. It is what it is. This is the first part of this example.

2.15   The second part is its reception. A gift has been given. What is your response?

2.16   The sunset is part of your human experience. In the lower order of that experience it speaks to your survival needs. It may signal many things, ranging from a desire to get safely home before it is dark, to a desire to eat an evening meal. It signals change in the natural world around you. Birds and squirrels and flowers too have a reaction to the setting of the sun. They react to what is. This is their response, an altogether lovely response of created to creator.

2.17   To rise above this lower order of experience is to receive and to give back. First the sunset is experienced for what it is. It is acknowledged. It is a fact of your existence as a human being, a part of the natural world, a gift of the Creator. Secondly, it is experienced relationally. It speaks to you and you to it. It binds you to the natural world and to the present, but also to the higher world and the eternal. It binds you to all those who have and will experience the sunset by being a shared experience. It is not there for you alone, but in listening to its call for a response, it becomes a gift for you that is in no way diminished by it being a gift for all.

2.18   Finally, the sunset becomes, through your experience of it, an opportunity to apply the art of thought.

2.19   These are the basic rules of the art of thought: First, to experience what is and to acknowledge what is, both as a fact of your existence as a human being and as a gift of the Creator. Second, to acknowledge the relationship inherent in the experience, the call for a response, and the nature of all gifts as being given to all.

2.20   While this may seem somewhat elementary in relation to a sunset, its application to all areas of life will at first seem quiet demanding. But what is elementary remains elementary once it is learned.

2.21   To experience what is and to acknowledge what is, one must be present, present as a human being. To experience what *is* and to acknowledge what *is* as being a gift of God is to be present as a divine being having a human experience. No part of being is negated. All senses and feelings of the human being are called into awareness and yet there is also acknowledgement of the Creator behind the created.

2.22   To acknowledge the relationship and the nature of the gift is to realize unity. To realize the call for a response is to hear the call to create like unto the Creator. This creating like unto the Creator may be used as a definition for the art of thought.

chapter 3

the Call to the Miracle

3.1   The first opportunities for the art of thought to be applied relate to memory in terms of your experience here. In other words they will relate to the re-experiencing of all that you believe has shaped your life. These opportunities are but the forerunners of new learning. They are but opportunities to replace illusion with the truth so that the truth of who you are is all that remains.

3.2   Seeing how different from the experience of illusion is the experience of truth is the same as seeing how different the art of thought is from the thinking of the ego-mind! The art of thought is diametrically opposed to the thinking of the ego-mind.

3.3   The ego-mind sees nothing for what it is. The ego-mind sees not anything but what it *wants* as gifts and even these it sees not as gifts but as rewards. The ego-mind barters rather than giving and receiving as one, believing in a return only for effort. Because it sees only rewards and not gifts, it cannot see that gifts are shared. Because it cannot see that gifts are shared, it cannot afford to see relationship. Because it believes it is *on its own* it cannot see the higher order. Because of all of this, it cannot experience the truth and so exists in illusion.

3.4   The experience of truth dispels illusion and thus the ego-mind. The art of thought replaces the ego-mind with the wholehearted. The wholehearted is but the heart and mind joined in unity.

13

3.5   How can what is closely guarded extend? How can what is controlled create? How can what continues to give in to fear know love? All your reasons for fear-based living have been discounted one by one. And yet you dare not try to live without it. Why? Because of the thoughts of the ego-mind. The ego-mind is concerned only with its own survival but it has you convinced it is your survival that depends on it. How can you be convinced to live as if the truth were otherwise? For only if you begin to live as if the truth were otherwise can you see that it truly is other-wise, or based on a wisdom other than what has come before.

3.6   The only way for you to come to live in truth is through faith — not a faith in what might be — but a faith in what is. A faith in what is, is a faith in miracles. Miracles are what you are now asked to call upon. Calling upon miracles is an act of faith. You think the quest for miracles is a quest for proof that demonstrates a lack of faith but the reverse is true. What kind of miracle would lead to a lack of faith? There is no such kind of miracle.

3.7   I ask you now to request a miracle.

3.8   What kind of a miracle should you ask for? How big of a miracle should you request? How big is your faith? How much proof does it require? I speak not in jest but ask you to seriously consider just what kind of miracle is needed to get you to change your mind about who you are and about the nature of your thoughts.

3.9   Observe yourself as you think through this question. Can you remove all fear from it? Why should it be that fear is what you encounter? The bigger the miracle that occurs to you, the more you are likely to fear the consequences. These are not consequences for the world you fear, but consequences for yourself. If you requested a miracle, and it came true, what then? If you request a small miracle and it comes true, how awful you would feel that you had not requested a bigger miracle. You will almost feel panic at the thought of such a choice being put before you. If you will agree to choose a miracle at all, which many of you will balk at doing, you want to choose the "right" miracle. Some of you may think through just what kind of miracle would be most convincing to you since you see this exercise as what it is, an attempt to convince you to think otherwise about yourself. If you ask for a cure for a disease, how will you know that this cure is a miracle and not the result of scientific discovery or the natural course an illness was bound to take? What miracle could be seen as only miracle and not leave doubt as to its circumstances? Would you choose, however, a miracle that would leave no room for doubt? Such a simple miracle might be the turning of water into wine. What harm could come from it? And yet even this you would fear for if you asked for such a miracle and it came to be, you would then have to contemplate your power to perform miracles. Here you find your greatest fear of all — fear of your power.

3.10 Willingness does not require conviction but leads to conviction. The apostles had no faith in their ability to perform miracles. The faith they showed was in their willingness to try. This little willingness gave way to conviction as miracles flowed through them as the blessings that they are.

3.11 I do not want to lose any of you here, but such is your fear that you can already see your own loss. As great as the fear of miracles is, the fear of not being able to perform is greater. You think of this as a test and one you can pass or fail. And what's more, not only would your passing of this test require you to contemplate your power, but your failure would require you to contemplate your lack of it. If you asked for a miracle and it did not come to be, wouldn't it negate all you have achieved thus far and send you back to a state of disbelief?

Better not to try at all than to risk trying and failing when such consequences would seem to hang in the balance.

3.12   But again I tell you this is no idle request. Whatever is necessary to convince you now is what I will provide. Such is the urgency of the time, the urgency for the return to unity, the urgency of the need to leave fear behind. Can you not, from this one example of your fear of miracles, see the glaring reality of all you still would fear?

3.13   This too is a means of unlearning. How can you leave behind all you fear without seeing all you fear for what it is and choosing to lay it aside?

3.14   This does not have to be done right now if your fear is mightier than your willingness. But hold this thought within your mind. What is needed to convince you will be provided. Such is the urgency of your return to unity. If not now, then soon, you will be asked to make this final choice, this choice to leave fear behind for good and to become who you are.

3.15   Who you are is a miracle worker. This is not all that you are but is a measure of who you are. This is not all that you are but this is the quickest means of realizing who you are. As was said in *A Course in Miracles*, miracles are timesaving devices. Although asking you to choose a miracle would seem to violate one of the rules of miracle-readiness as described in *A Course in Miracles*, the extreme need of your return to love requires extreme measures.

3.16   Let us consider your objections to miracles one-by-one for in so doing we will uncover the source of all your fears as well as the Source of miracles.

3.17   First you will say you have no objections to miracles, only to having them performed through you. Your lack of willingness to perform miracles, you will say, stems from your unworthiness to perform miracles. Your unworthiness stems from your belief that you are "only" human. You are not God. You are not a holy person. Thus miracles should not flow through you.

3.18   Secondly you would object to being asked to choose a miracle. Surely you cannot know the consequences of what any miracle would have on the rest of the world. If you were to ask for a life to be spared, how would you know it was not that person's "time to die?" If you were to ask for the cure of a disease, how would you know that disease was not meant to be to further someone's learning? If you were to ask to win the lottery, how could such selfishness not be punished?

3.19   Thirdly, you might, at the suggestion that you need proof to shore up your faith, balk, even while you remain convinced that a failure of such proof would shake your faith.

3.20   Fourth, you might resist the suggestion that God would grant miracles on such a whim, such a fanciful idea as that of you being convinced of your own power. How could this possibly be important? Even were you to possess such power, surely it is a power that is of God and needs not you for its accomplishment. Better not to mess with such things. Even the thought of it leads you to ideas of magic and power that is not of this world and thus that must have a dark side as well as a light side. Here suspicion dawns and threatens all you have come to hold dear.

3.21   These thoughts border on the sacrilegious. Miracles are the realm of Jesus and of the saints and that is surely where they belong. To even implore them would be heresy.

3.22   You fear as well that you do not know what miracles are and so cannot perform them. You want a definition first. What is an appropriate miracle? For whom should they be requested? What are the criteria? How are they done? Do they happen all at once? Or can they be for some future date? What about the correction of something that has already occurred? You have far too many questions without answers to choose a miracle.

3.23   Although many more fears might prevail upon you, we will consider only one further fear, the fear of making the wrong choice in your choice of miracles. This is the same as a fear of scarcity. For surely the working of one miracle would be a fluke, proof of nothing and easily discounted and explained away. Surely to believe that where one miracle worked another might be possible would be to have ideas of grandeur not meant for you. Here your thoughts might stray to the performing of many miracles. What a media circus that would be. You would be in demand to end so much suffering in so many places. Surely you wouldn't want that even if it could come to be. Indeed this would require the auspices of a saintly soul and not one such as you.

3.24   See you not the choices made in each of these scenarios and the reasoning or lack of reasoning behind them? You are not worthy. You are not saintly, godlike or even holy. You might choose incorrectly. You might invoke retribution. You might be selfish. You might be proved to have no faith. You might succumb to thoughts of grandeur.

3.25   In short, you are too afraid, for a variety of reasons, to try. In short, you are not willing and have many reasons for not being willing. What we have done here is bring your fears to light, fears that you did not even realize you held so closely or would be so terrified to let go.

3.26   Now we can address each of these fears, bringing to them the art of thought rather than the thinking of the ego-mind.

chapter 4

the Center of the Universe

4.1   By asking you to request a miracle, I am honoring who you are and inviting you into the state of mind that is miracle-readiness. The art of thought *is* the expression of that state. The art of thought *is* the miracle.

4.2   Thus we must dispel, with the illusion of fear, the illusion of specificity. You have not been asked to request a specific miracle. Although your thoughts have naturally gone to consideration of the specific, this is but an indication that you are still in the habit of thinking that you learned under the instruction of the ego-mind. This Treatise must change that habit in order for all of your thoughts to become the miracles that express the truth of who you are. This Treatise will put your instruction fully under my guidance and allow you to disregard the instruction of the ego-mind.

4.3   *A Course of Love* began with an injunction to pray. *A Course in Miracles* began with a definition of miracles. Both are the same. Prayer and the art of thought are the same. This should serve to make it clear that the request I have made of you is once again far more broad and generalizable than your old habit of thought has led you to see. Miracles are, in other words, a way of thinking, the new way that we are going to learn together. They are the state of giving and receiving as one. They are the state in which blessings flow. They are your natural state.

4.4   How can the rules of thought we have identified serve to bring about the miracle that you are? The first means identified was that of experiencing what *is* and acknowledging what *is* both as a fact of your existence as a human being and as a gift of the Creator. Now that we have more properly identified the miracle, you must see that your Self is what is in need of identification and acknowledgment. This identification and acknowledgment was the stated goal of *A Course of Love*. It does not negate your existence as a human being nor does it deny your existence as being a gift of the Creator. Recall the sunset. Are you any less the glory of God than the sun? This is a call to be as aware of your Self as you are capable of being aware of the sunset.

4.5   When the sun has remained but an object to you, no effect is possible from the sunset. The sun, even during the most blazing sunset, has at times remained no more than an object. So too has your self. When your self is seen as no more than a body it is seen as little more than an object.

4.6   The second rule of the art of thought is to acknowledge relationship, the call for a response, and the nature of all gifts as being given to all. This is a call to realize that *you* exist in relationship, that *your* relationship calls for a response, and that *you* are given to all as all are given to you.

4.7   This is an enormous shift in your habit of thought as *you* become the center of the universe.

4.8   This is quite a different *you* than the self of the ego-mind. The ego-mind, in its imitation of creation, put the you of the ego or the body at the center of its thought system and from this central position developed all of its ideas of glorifying the separated self as well as of subjugating the separated self. This subjugation to the ego-mind is what led to the ego-mind being able to develop the "laws of man." These laws of man are the laws of the body's survival.

4.9   Your responsibilities shift completely under the laws of God. Your thoughts are released from their concentration on what exists outside of you as your responsibility is placed where it belongs, in the call to respond. This response is only yours to give and is all you are asked to give. This response comes from within the Self — the rightly identified and acknowledged Self.

4.10   Think of all you now feel responsible for and this lesson will become more clear. While your first thoughts will automatically go to a lengthy list of those concerns associated with the survival of the body, they will miss a whole aspect of concerns associated with keeping others other. You keep others "other" by attempting to respond for them rather than responding to them. You have thought that it is your responsibility to care for the world outside of yourself rather than for your Self.

4.11   There is much play on the words response/responsible/and responsibility here. This is no accident. Your call is to respond and you have seen this call incorrectly as a call to be responsible. The idea of responsibility sprang from the ego-mind that would usurp the power of God. What kind of gift arrives with a demand for the receiver to be responsible for it?

4.12   You may answer that there are many, even within this course's definition of gift, the most obvious of which might be your children — another might be your talents. It is the idea of your responsibility for these gifts that has led to your oppression. Again I tell you, your call is to respond rather than to be responsible. How can you be free to respond when your thinking remains tied to responsibility?

4.13   Responsibility but implies a guardianship that is not needed. Responsibility implies needs that would not be met without you. Response is given and thus is genuine. It is a natural act of giving and receiving as one. Responsibility is a

21

demanded response, a necessary response, an obligation. Response happens from within. Responsibility is all about dealing with an outside world. That both may result in the same or similar actions does not negate the need for the difference to be realized. Charity is a responsibility. Love is a response. See you not the difference? Can a father not be guided by responsibility and still fail to give love? Can a dancer not struggle mightily to perfect her talent without experiencing its joy?

4.14   Do you think the Creator is responsible for what was created? To think of the Creator in this way is to think of the Creator with the upside-down thinking of the ego-mind. Is this not the kind of thinking that has caused you to blame God for what you have labeled "bad" as well as to praise God for that which you have labeled "good?" Would not this kind of a creator be at odds with the concept of free will?

4.15   But for a creator not to respond to what has been created — this would indeed be a travesty! This would be antithetical to the laws of creation! This would be antithetical to love!

4.16   My request to you to choose a miracle is but a request to you to hear Creation's response to who you are. What might such a response sound like? Feel like? Look like? It is a response of pure appreciation and love. It is always available. It is the gift given in everything you look upon and see without the obstacle of the ego-mind's interpretation.

4.17   Let us speak a moment of this interpretation. That each of you interprets what you see, read, hear, smell and touch differently must mean something. What you have decided this means is that you are an independent thinker, something you have prized. Some of you will accept another's interpretation of meaning if it is helpful to you, saves you time, or seems in accord with your own views. Others of you feel it necessary to interpret everything "on your own." Without further discussion, you would see interpretation and response quite similarly and this would but lead to a continuation of the belief in different forms of the truth.

4.18 The art of thought is being taught here in order to prevent just such a conclusion. The truth is the truth and not dependent upon your definition of it. A response is not an interpretation. A response is an expression of who *you* are rather than of what you believe something else to be.

4.19 You who have thought that your interpretation of events and feelings has given them their meaning – think again. Their meaning exists already and is not up to you to determine. This is not your responsibility. You who have thought that your interpretation of situations and the feelings they have aroused have defined who you are – think again. Be willing to apply the art of thought rather than the thinking of the ego-mind. Interpretation but gives you opinions *about* those things that you experience. Response reveals the truth to you because it reveals the truth *of you*.

4.20 The joy you have thought has come to you from an interpretation that is uniquely your own is as nothing compared to the joy that will come to you from a response that is uniquely *you*. But you must give up your penchant for interpretation before you can learn to respond. I realize that this will concern you while you continue to not realize the difference between response and interpretation. The only way for this concern to have the chance to leave you is for you to begin to practice the art of thought and begin to learn the difference.

4.21 The first opportunities for you to learn the art of thought will be provided through what we have called the re-experiencing of memory. These are opportunities to re-experience the lessons your life has brought you. You will experience the same lessons in the same way, rather than in a *new* way, if you meet these experiences again with the attitude of interpreting them rather than responding to them. They do not require interpretation but response. Response was what was required in the first place and your inability to respond need not be repeated. You are being revisited with these lessons expressly for the purpose of *not* repeating your former reaction or interpretation of them. You are being revisited with these lessons so that you may apply to them the art of thought rather than the thinking of the ego-mind. The art of thought will reveal the truth to you. The thinking of the ego-mind would simply reinterpret the meaning you previously gave to these lessons.

4.22 This is a sticky distinction, for you are used to congratulating yourself on the maturity required to reinterpret previous lessons. To form a new opinion about something gives you a feeling of open-mindedness and growth. Lay aside your desire for reasons for self-congratulation in favor of self-revelation. The saying, "The truth shall be revealed to you" is the same as saying "Your Self shall be revealed to you."

4.23 *Revelation* is a proper description of the mode by which the art of thought teaches and helps you learn. It is not through study, effort, or re-interpretation but through revelation.

4.24 Revelation is direct communication with God in the sense that it is direct communication from a Self you have known not, the Self that is one with the Creator.

4.25 We must backtrack a little here to do the same exposition that we did in regard to miracles in regard to revelation. By asking you to choose a miracle, you were provided a means through which your fears became clear to you. There are a few of you who would deny these fears. Fewer still are unafraid of miracles and eager to embrace them.

As you may have surmised, we are getting at your final fears here, those most deeply buried and kept in secret from you. Some of you who would count yourselves least fearful are those of you whose fears are most deeply buried. So whether you count yourself among the fearful or not, please continue to give me your attention just a while longer as we uncover all that would still hold you back.

4.26   As was said within *A Course of Love*, all fear is doubt about your self. Now we must expand upon this thought, for doubt about your self is doubt about God. While God is nothing but the Source of Love, you have, in your doubt, made of God the source of fear. Pause a moment here and let the enormity of this confusion sink in, for this is the reversal in thinking that will pave the way for all the rest. Because of this confusion you have responded to Creation with fear. Is it no wonder a new response is asked of you?

4.27   In the translations of the Bible and many other religious texts, the word or idea of awe has been confused with the word or idea of fear. *A Course in Miracles* told you that awe is the providence of God and not due miracles or any other thing or being. I bring this up to assure you that this confusion is nothing new, but a confusion so deeply ingrained in you that it has become an aspect of your self as a human being. From time immemorial, fear has been associated with God. This was the thinking I came to reverse. While I succeeded in revealing a God of love, this revelation has not been reconciled with your experience here. This is what we will now seek to do by putting an end to fear and ushering in, with this ending, the beginning of a time of miracles.

chapter 5

the Choice for Love

5.1   Why, when a God of Love was revealed so long ago and in so many times and in so many forms since then that they remain forever countless, has fear of God remained? The only answer possible is because fear of the self has remained.

5.2   This is a two-fold fear that must be looked at carefully now and with all the power of the art of thought. One aspect of this fear has to do with the human experience, the other aspect with the divine experience.

5.3   When it was said within *A Course of Love* that the great paradox of creation is that, while creation is perfect, something has gone wrong within it, this fear in relation to the human experience is of what it was I spoke. The choice for suffering that has been made within the human condition is what I speak of specifically here. While I can tell you suffering is illusion, you cannot still your fear of it nor tear your eyes away from it or remove from it the feelings of your heart. While I came to reveal the choice of love to you, the choice that you each must make to end such suffering, the illusion of suffering has continued and in its continuation made the choice of love seem all but impossible. If not for the suffering that you see all around you, the choice for love would have been made. If the choice for love had been made, the suffering you see around you would be no more. This is the paradox. The second aspect of this fear is fear of the divine. A part of this fear of the divine is related to the fear of the human condition. How can you not be fearful of creation when such suffering occurs within it? But there is another aspect that relates to the fear of union we spent much time discussing within this course. It is a fear of the human mind that cannot comprehend the all or the nothingness, the eternal or the void. While your thought system here has been described often as insanity, this is the insanity you would fear and a fear that may actually grow stronger as you get closer to the truth. This is the part of you that believes this communication itself is insane, that believes that to contemplate miracles is insane, that both welcomes and fears visions and abilities you see as being currently beyond your capabilities.

5.5   This fear of all and nothingness is fear of God, fear of life, fear of creation, fear of self. For there is only all and nothing.

5.6   A part of you is aware of this and as fearful of the all of everything as of the void of nothing. You feel as if you are headed toward "something" from somewhere but neither here nor there feel completely real to you. The lucky among you have made of this in between place an adventure, and are happy in your seeking. You do not care to end this happy state and there is indeed much to be learned from the in between. It is, however, a starting point only.

5.7   The whole of life could in fact be seen as the illusion of an *in between* you have created between all and nothing. This in between place is your comfort zone. Although you feel compelled to push at its edges, this pushing not only leaves the edges quite intact, but causes them to be capable of offering resistance. Your search for something within the in between, if it leads not beyond the in between, shields you from the recognition of the all you are capable of finding and the nothing in which you reside.

5.8   In order to experience the truth, you must move into a state that is real. *Nothing* is as real as *everything*, and is what some of you will experience or have experienced as a "dark night of the soul." To realize that you reside in nothingness is but the counterpart of realizing that there is an all to which you belong.

5.9   Again I tell you that it is only your body and the thinking of your ego-mind that make the in between state of the illusion in which you now exist seem real. I must make a distinction here, however, between the seemingly real and the aspect of your existence that *is* real. Your heart as we have defined it many times within this Course, must exist in the thought system that is real to you. The thought system of the ego-mind is what has been real to you and is where your heart has been held captive. Thus, your real Self is not present in the realm of the truly real, but is actually present within the illusion. This is why all seeking must turn within, toward the heart where the real Self abides. There is nothing else that will free who you are but freedom from the ego's thought system. That the ego's thought system has kept you from this freedom is the seeming difficulty you experience in learning this course of study and the reason, when you have freed yourself, that you will look back and see how easy this one choice really is.

5.10   The body, and the "you" whom you think you are, would not experience anything without the presence of the heart. The heart is the only cause of your *experience* here. When released from the ego thought system, the heart becomes the determiner of what you experience since you know it as the *cause*. This is what is meant by mind and heart being joined in union, or being wholehearted. It is the *real* you or center of your Self, being joined with the only thought system that is real, the thought system of the truth. How could a thought system based on anything but the truth lead to anything but illusion?

5.11   The "here" that you experience is the experience dictated by the ego-mind, and this experience is all that makes you believe you are other than who you are. The abolishing of the ego-mind, as stated many times and in many ways, must now be brought to completion.

5.12   This is why I have asked you to choose the manner in which you would be once and finally convinced. You must *experience* the reality of the new thought system or it will remain forever theoretical. You must let go of the foundation of fear on which the old thought system was built in order to *experience* the new.

5.13   The art of thought *invites* the *experience* of the new thought system by being willing to replace the old with the new. While this will at first be a learned activity, and as such have its moments of seeming difficulty, it is learned only in the sense of your practice of the mindfulness that will allow the memory of it to return to you.

5.14   Mindfulness and wholeheartedness are but different expressions of the union of mind and heart. Mindfulness will aid you in remembering. Wholeheartedness will aid you in reconciling the laws of God with the laws of man. Through mindfulness you will remember who you are. Through wholeheartedness you will be who are.

5.15   It is in this way that you will enter a time of miracles, put an end to suffering, and begin the return to love.

chapter 6

the Act of Prayer

6.1   The thought system of the ego-mind is a learned system and this is why it can be unlearned. The thought system of the truth is always present, as the truth is always present, and can be neither learned nor unlearned. The truth will be revealed to you as soon as the learned thought system ceases to block its realization.

6.2   How is this revelation to take place? It will begin by learning the art of thought as the act of prayer. We have spoken already of memory here, and have presented the acts of reproducing and recollecting that are involved with memory as acts of creation. Prayer is but reproducing and recollecting a divine memory and divine memory cannot help but produce a divine outcome. Said in another way, prayer reproduces the truth and allows the truth to exist as it is. Prayer does this because it is the act of consciously choosing union. Choosing union moves you into the real state of "all" from the unreal state of the in between. Only from within a state that is real can anything happen in truth.

6.3   Prayer must be redefined as the act of consciously choosing union. With this definition, you can see how your life can become a prayer. This does not negate the fact that a prayer is also a constant dialogue of asking, being answered, and responding. This is the aspect of prayer that makes of it an act of creation.

6.4   Prayer and miracles work hand in hand once both are seen for what they are. Do not forget here, however, what union is. Union is the mind and heart being joined in wholeheartedness. It is *your* union with your *Self.* Union with your Self is union with God. Your concentration must not stray back to old concepts of prayer or of reaching God through the intercession of prayer as if God were separate from you and accessible only through a specific means of communication. You can see, perhaps, how this attitude toward prayer came about, as it is, like much you have learned, close to the truth without being the truth.

6.5   To *use* prayer only as a means of reaching out to a god seen as separate is to attempt to use what cannot be used. Such ideas of prayer have had credence because this reaching out does at least recognize that there is something to reach out to. Such ideas of prayer have long been opening doors for those who are ready to walk through them to a real relationship with God and Self. But this is not the concept of prayer of which we speak nor one that can reasonably be called a way of life or likened to the art of thought. Prayers such as these emanate from either heart or mind and have not the power of the wholehearted. Prayers such as these emanate from the state of fear that is the reality of the separated self.

6.6   To pray out of fear is not to pray at all, because such prayer chooses not the union that is the prerequisite. To pray out of fear is to ask from an unreal state of lack for what is seen as missing or desired. In contrast, true prayer, formed in union, is a means of creating, recollecting, or recalling a divine memory and transforming that divine memory into a present moment experience.

6.7   Memory is valuable to us now because it relies not on perception. If perception were all that were available to you, each experience would begin and end and have no ability to relate to anything else at all. Without memory, what you learned one day would be gone the next. A person you met one day you would not know the next. Memory allows relationship. Memory, or how you relate to past experiences, is what makes each individual unique. A family can share many similar experiences without relating to them in the same way. It is the way experience is related to, through memory, which shapes the different personalities, paths, and future experiences of each of you.

6.8   So what happens when memories of past experiences are revisited under the all- encompassing umbrella of a new way of thought?   The different personalities become one, the different paths become one path, the future experiences become one. And in this oneness is peace everlasting.

6.9   When this oneness is accomplished divine memories arise to replace perception. This is miracle-mindedness. The accomplishment of this state of being is what you are here for. It is your return to your Self. It heralds the return of heaven through the second coming of Christ, the energy that will bridge the two worlds.

chapter 7

the New Learning

7.1   Suffering is seen as a condition of this world because the world is seen as a world in which who you are can never be accomplished. You have perceived this inability to be who you are in terms of not being able to do as you would desire to do, live as you would desire to live, achieve what you would choose to achieve. The true way in which to see this prerequisite to the condition of suffering is as the perceived inability to be who you truly are, a being existing in union. Take away all, for the moment, that you would strive to be, and the feeling of not being able to be accomplished or complete will still be with you. Recall the many times you felt certain that a particular achievement would complete you and would take away your feelings of lack. Even the most successful among you have found that your worldly success has been unable to bring you the satisfaction and the peace you desire.

7.2   Even the most spiritual and godly among you accept suffering. Even those who understand as completely as possible the truth of who they are accept suffering. My use of the word *accept* is important here, as these may not see suffering as pain but only as a natural part of being human that calls for acceptance. They thus find peace within suffering rather than abolishing suffering. This acceptance is due to the belief that spirit has chosen a form, and more accurately put a "lesser" form in which to exist, and that this choice includes the choice to suffer. This belief may accept suffering as a learning devise rather than a punishment, but it still, in its acceptance of a false notion, invites suffering. This belief accepts learning through contrast, that evil is seen in relation to good, peace in relation to chaos, love in relation to fear. This belief exists in the in between, where on the one hand there is darkness, and on the other hand there is light. One or the other must exist at a given time, but never both. Thus the absence of good health is disease; the absence of peace is conflict; the absence of truth is illusion. This belief does not accept that there is only one reality and that it must exist where you are.

7.3   We are moving you now away from all such beliefs to a knowing that precludes the need for belief at all.

7.4   Yes, I have said that contrast is a favored teaching devise of the Holy Spirit. But I have not yet said that the time of the Holy Spirit is ending even though I have stated that the time of the second coming of Christ is here. I have said that the time of parables has ended and asked you not to look to those historical figures that taught in such a way as your examples any longer. I have said a new way of learning is needed and is here. To continue to rely on the ways of old, *no matter how effective they were and no matter how much they spoke the truth* will be to not learn the new.

7.5   You have advanced, taken steps, climbed to a new level, and acquired an ability to perceive differently in order to make this new learning possible. If you do not let what you have attained serve you, you will not realize what this new learning has been for. You may reach an ideal of human satisfaction and happiness, but you will not go beyond what is human.

7.6   This is why we must speak now of being human in a new way. We must reconcile the differences between the human and divine. We must, in other words, speak of incarnation.

chapter 8

Incarnation and Resurrection

8.1   I was proclaimed to be the Word incarnate, the union of the human and the divine, the manifestation of the Will of God.   I have told you that you are no different than I was. Now I call you to be no different than I am.

8.2   As a man, I suffered, died and was buried.   As who I Am, I resurrected.   "I am the resurrection and the life."   What I was in life was the manifestation, in form, of the Will of God. So too have you been.   God is the giver of life, thus life is God's Will.   But with my resurrection, which was accomplished for all, the meaning of life, the reality of life, changed, though you have known this not.   The great experiment in separation ended with the resurrection, though you have known this not. For the resurrection and life are now one and the same.

8.3   That they *are* the same has not meant the automatic realization of this change of enormous proportions.   The very nature of change is one of slow realization.   Change occurs all around you every day without your realization of it.   Only in retrospect are the greatest of changes seen.   The understanding of the truth of an historical event changes over time and it may take a hundred or a thousand or even two thousand years for the *real* truth to be realized.   Even though many versions of the truth have been accepted previously, there is only one truth. There was only one truth at the time the event or change took place, and there is only one truth in time or eternity regardless of the variety of interpretations of the truth.

8.4   I have come to you now to reveal the one truth that has existed for the past two thousand years without your comprehension of it. The nature of life changed with the resurrection. *I am the resurrection and the life. So are you.*

8.5   As I no longer suffer the separation, you need no longer suffer the separation. Even though the resurrection returned not life to the form I once occupied, it returned me to you in the form of the resurrected Christ who exists in all of you, bringing resurrection even unto your forms. I became the Word incarnate upon my resurrection rather than upon my birth. This will seem confusing given your definition of incarnation as the Word made flesh. You took this to mean that flesh took on the definition of the Word or the Almighty when I became flesh and bone through birth. But neither my birth nor my death were consequent with the Word as the Word is I Am, the Word is Life Eternal. My resurrection brought about the Word made flesh in each of you. You who have come after me are not as I was but as I Am. Does this not make sense, even in your human terms of evolution? *You are the resurrected and the life.*

8.6   How does this relate to your thinking? You have been reborn as god-man, as God and man united. The resurrection is the cause and effect of the union of the human and divine. This *is* accomplished. This is *in effect* the way in which the man Jesus became the Christ. This is *in effect* the way.

8.7   Now, how could one man's resurrection be the way or even *a way*. How can resurrection provide a path or example for you to follow? You must see the link between resurrection and incarnation, the link between resurrection and the birth of the god-man.

8.8   The heart and mind joined in union accomplished the reunion of the separated self with God. The resurrection was evidence of this accomplishment. It laid aside death's claim and with it the claim of all that is temporary. The resurrection was witnessed as the proof required, much as proof has been offered to you now in the form of miracles. How could one rise from the dead and others not follow?

8.9   Illusion is the death you need but arise from. Arise and awaken to your resurrected self! There is no longer a *god-head* to follow into paradise. Take not the example of any of these and know instead the example of woman, of Mary, Mother of God.

8.10   What is a mother but she who incarnates, makes spirit flesh through her own flesh, makes spirit flesh through union. That you have, in your version of creation, made it necessary for woman to join with man in order for new life to come forth, is but another example of how your memory of creation was made to serve what you would have come to be. The separated self could not exist alone and so created a way in which other separated forms could come into existence and live with it in separation.   This recognition of union as a prerequisite to creation is proof of your memory's tenacity and the failure of illusion to completely rid you of what you know.

8.11   The virgin birth was a necessary step in the re-claiming of the real act of creation, the bringing forth of the new through union with the divine Self. Whether you believe the virgin birth was reality or myth matters not, as myth and reality have no concrete distinction in the illusion within which you live. In other words you live as much by myth as by truth and myth often more accurately reflects the truth than what you would call real. This is not a call, however, to embrace myth, but to embrace the truth.

8.12   Mary is called upon now as the myth to end all myths for in this example life alone is the key to the riddle provided.

8.13   You are each called to return to your virgin state, to a state unaltered by the separation, a state in which what is begotten is begotten through union with God. It is from this unaltered state that you are free to resurrect, as I resurrected. It is through the Blessed Virgin Mary's resurrection *in form* that the new pattern of life is revealed.

8.14   The new pattern of life is the ability to resurrect in form. The ability to resurrect in life. The ability to resurrect now.

8.15   Thus is the glory that is yours returned to you *in life* rather than *in death*.

8.16   The male provided the manifestation or the effect of the cause created by the female in the virgin birth. My mother, Mary, was responsible for the incarnation of Christ in me as I am responsible for the incarnation of Christ in you. This union of the male and female is but union of the parts of yourself expressed in form and story, expressed, in other words, in a visual pattern that aides your understanding of the invisible. It is one more demonstration of the union that returns you to your natural state. It is one more demonstration of cause and effect being one in truth. It is one more demonstration of what needs to occur now, in this time, in order for the truth of the resurrection to be revealed and lived.

8.17   We have talked thus far of union of heart and mind. Lest you think that this union is not all encompassing, we will reflect a moment here on how the art of thought brings all you have seen as parts of the self, such as male and female, conception and action, inspiration and manifestation, together into the wholehearted.

chapter 9

Giving and Receiving

9.1   The art of thought is not possible without a return to the virgin or unaltered self. The *practice* of the art of thought is what will complete the return begun through the course work in *A Course of Love*. This will bring about the union of the male and female, of conception and action, of inspiration and manifestation. This is what we have been speaking of when speaking of miracle-mindedness or miracle-readiness. This *is* wholeheartedness and is achieved through mindfulness.

9.2   Whether you be male or female matters not as you are in truth the union of each. The end of separation that brought about the resurrection, brought about this union, and the separation of male and female continues to exist only in form.

9.3   However, we are talking now, in a certain sense, of an elevation of form. While this is actually an elevation beyond form, it must begin in the reality where you think you are. In other words, it must begin with form. You cannot await some changed state but must create the changed state you await.

9.4   You are used to creating in outward ways. One of the few exceptions to this outward creation is the act of giving birth. But birth, like all outward manifestations, but reflects inner change. The growth of a new being within the womb of another is a visible manifestation of gestation, which is the prelude to resurrection. What was once part of the mother and father, what would have died without the joining that occurred within, becomes new life.

9.5   Now you are asked to carry new life not in the womb but in the united mind and heart.

9.6   Let us consider why birth has been the purview of women and why men have been incapable of giving birth. This is because, in your version of creation, there needed to be a giver and a receiver. You knew that giving and receiving makes *one* in truth. This is your recreation of this universal truth. You remembered that something does not come from nothing and that nothing is all that exists without relationship.

9.7   You have not remembered that the first union is of mind and heart. The first union is union with the Self. Union with the Self is resurrection or rebirth. All are capable of this life-giving union. All are capable of birthing the Self.

9.8   But what then of the necessary act of giving and receiving? In this birth of the Self, who is the giver and who is the receiver? In order for the Self to be birthed, giving and receiving must be one in truth. Yet it seems there must be one to give and one to receive. You have long waited to receive what you have thought could come only from some *other*. Your churches are but evidence of this as you seek from religion an intercessor, one to facilitate for you this receiving or communion. Only through the Christ *within you* does this giving and receiving become one in truth.

9.9   As I awaited my death I was given the gift of knowing what would come to be through my resurrection. This I tried to pass on in the simplest of terms. I tried to make it known that while I would die and resurrect into a new form, you would also. I made it known that this new form would exist within you, that you would become the Body of Christ, and that giving and receiving would be complete.

9.10   You are the Body of Christ.

9.11   What will it mean to bring about the union of the male and female, of conception and action, of inspiration and manifestation? It will mean union and a time of miracles. It will mean that you are the living Body of Christ.

9.12   In the broadest of terms, this is already happening. As the ego has become threatened and allowed the coming of guidance, males and females both have begun to work with the parts of themselves over which the ego has the least control. For males this has most often meant a turning away from the intellectual realm, which was ruled by the ego, to the realm of feelings. For females this has most often meant a turning away from the feeling realm where their egos held most sway, toward the intellectual. This instinctual turning toward an opposite has been made to serve you through the intercession of the Holy Spirit. In turning within rather than without to find what you need to free you from the ego's reign, you have turned toward wholeness. In the same way that embracing both the male and female attributes within you causes a merging of both and a wholeness to be achieved, so too does a wholeness then come about with conception and action, inspiration and manifestation.

9.13   Lest you fight these ideas as stereotypical, I will give just a few brief examples. These I ask you to cull from your own recent experience. What has caused the ego to become more apparent to you as you have learned this course? Has it not seemed to lie dormant for periods of time and then to suddenly be called back to life through some event or situation? What was this event or situation? Did it not threaten your self-image? And did this threat occur at what you would call the feeling level or at the intellectual level? Were your feelings hurt or your pride? Your feelings called into question or your ideas? And what guise did the ego take as it rallied to your aid? Did it require you to retreat or advance? Did it stir emotions or attempt to still them?

41

9.14   These may be difficult questions to answer as your initial reaction and your response will likely have taken on different forms. You may for instance, have reacted by being hurt or angry. Your response may then have been either an emotional one or an intellectual one. The point here is that the one that is most comfortable and that is likely your first reaction, is cognizant with your old pattern, or the pattern of the ego. What breaks the ego's hold will be the second reaction, or the turning away from the old.

9.15   One first reaction might be to puff oneself up with pride, bolster one's position, think one's way through, argue, manipulate, or chastise another so that you feel better in relationship to the other in the situation or event. Another's first reaction might be one of self-pity, of making oneself or another feel guilty, or of experiencing a sense of diminished self-esteem or worthiness. The first will feel like an intellectual position. The second like a feeling position. Turning away from the intellectual position to one of feeling will most readily and quickly solve the first. The second will be most readily and quickly overcome by a turn toward reason or the intellect. The perceived attack will have entered where you have placed your highest value and are most vulnerable. In the past your response would have been to protect and use that which you have most valued. Now your response will have been changing. You will not see so much to value in what has called your ego into action and will turn away from it.

9.16   What "was" is being thrown out and the first step in this is embracing what you heretofore have not embraced. You are pulling forth sides of yourself that were previously undervalued rather than looking for an *other* to provide what you lack. This is important and universal in its impact. It would seem to be about balance but is about wholeness. Male and female are labels laden with attributes. When the different attributes are merged, male and female will be no more and wholeness will reign.

chapter 10

Peace

10.1   Now let me address the issue of the peace you all have been experiencing as well as your reactions to this peace. It is so foreign to each of you that you can't quite imagine that it is what you are supposed to be feeling. There is a core of peace at the center of yourself now and the issues that you choose to deal with will not affect that core of peace at all. While you may find this almost disturbing, you will not go to extremes to break this peace.

10.2   My peace is yours. You have asked for it and it has been given to you. To not have it, you will have to choose not to have it. This will be tempting on occasion. You will wonder at the lack of extremes in your feelings and want to bring them back. You will experience this loss of extremes as a lack. You will think something is wrong. You will feel this particularly when others around you experience extremes. A friend is experiencing feelings on an extreme level and this will seem to tell you that this friend is really alive. Whether it be joy or sorrow, it will seem *real* in a way that peace does not. It will seem so *human* that a wave of desire to be fully human will wash over you. You will think that this human who has caught your attention is fully engaged and fully experiencing the moment. You will think this is what you want. And I say again that it will not matter whether it be joy or sorrow for you are, or have been, attracted by both for the same reason, the reason of wanting to be fully engaged in the human experience.

10.3   Here is this experience you have created and how often have you been fully engaged in it? How often have you given yourself over to those highs and lows? You will be tempted to give yourself over once again in this most human of ways. You will cry and laugh for the poignancy of the human experience. This is the *known* that you will be tempted not to give up. If you can't be moved from your peace by the greatest of these experiences, the most profound sorrow or the most all-encompassing joy, you will feel inhuman. You will think that this cannot be where you are meant to be, what you are meant to feel. You will wonder what is wrong with you.

10.4   This *is* temptation. The temptation of the human experience. This is what you continue to choose over the Peace of God. This is not a right or wrong choice but it is a choice. It is your free will to continue to make this choice.

10.5   You used your free will to choose the human experience. Now are you willing to use it to choose the Peace of God instead? Can you wholeheartedly choose peace? Can you choose peace long enough to become accustomed to joy without sorrow? If you cannot, you will continue to create hell as well as heaven and will continue the separation between the divine and the human. Is heaven worth enough to you to give up hell?

10.6   These extremes of the human experience have been learning devices. They have cracked open hearts and minds to the divine presence within. You have chosen them for just this reason. But you can now be an observer and look upon them as the learning choices of your brothers and sisters without choosing to return to learning in the same way again. You no longer need these experiences to alert you to the divine presence. Once you have learned to read you do not return to learning to read over and over again even while you may continue to read for a lifetime. You can continue to experience life and still carry the Peace of God within you. As you live in peace you can be an example to your brothers and sisters, an example that says there is another way.

10.7   Are you being asked to give up extremes? Yes. You are being asked to give up all that would take peace from you. But as you have been told before, you will be giving up nothing. It will seem as if it is so for a while perhaps. You will continue to be attracted to those living at the extremes and there is no reason not to take joy in observing another's happiness or to feel compassion at another's suffering. But you need not partake and you cannot partake if you are going to carry the Peace of God within you.

10.8   This is what has been meant by the many references that have been made to God not seeing suffering. God exists with you in peace. When you feel peace, you feel the Peace of God. There is no other peace. There is no other God. Whether you believe it now or not, I assure you, within the Peace of God is all the joy of what you have known as the human experience and none of the sorrow.

10.9   Each of you will have an experience you look back upon, an experience of profound joy or grief that also became an experience of profound learning. You will think that you would not be who you are now without experiences such as this one. You will think that I cannot possibly be asking you to give up these types of experiences. But you have already had them! I ask you not to give them up. Only to make now a new choice.

10.10   It is your memory of these events that hold such sway over you that you would choose not the Peace of God. But look past what you have remembered to what was truly there. No moment of true learning ever arrived without the Peace of God for without the Peace of God no true learning is possible.

10.11   Let us separate experiences you might call peak experiences from experiences of extremes that served as learning devices.   Peak experiences often follow occasions of happiness or trauma, but they do not happen within them. Peak experiences are what you can look forward to rather than back upon if you but choose the Peace of God.

10.12   The extremes that we are talking of leaving behind are extremes of reaction to a chosen lesson.   What you are being asked to leave behind is the need for such lessons.   If you have learned the curriculum, what further lessons are needed?   What quiet knowing cannot come to you in peace?   Why would you believe you can learn from the turmoil of extremes what you cannot learn in peace eternal?

10.13   This is what you have believed and why you have not chosen to accept your inheritance.   Yet let the memory of the truth return to you now and you will see that peace is all you have sought learning to attain.   If you do not pause now and accept that it is here, you will not know the Peace of God that is your own Self.

10.14   Peace, in whatever way you find it, in whatever expression it takes, no matter what words you use to describe it, is your answer to God and God's answer to you.   Peace is the inheritance I left you.   Peace of body, mind, and heart.   Peace is the realm of miracles, the condition of the wholehearted, the prerequisite to the art of thought, the description of heaven, the abode of Christ.   Peace has come to you and you to Peace.

10.15   Now your final instruction is here.   You who have found peace – live in peace.   You who have been given the Peace of God – go in Peace.   Spread peace throughout the land. Go out in peace and love and service to all.   For in this going out you come home and bring with you all the brothers and sisters you have brought to peace.   Go in peace to love and serve with all your heart. Thus are we one heart, one mind, one unity. Thus are we one in a relationship of love and peace that is our eternal home. Welcome home my brothers and sisters in Christ. Welcome home.

A Treatise on the
NATURE OF UNITY
AND ITS RECOGNITION

The Second Treatise

chapter 1

Treasure

1.1   You are all aware, at least at times, that there are
treasures that lie within you.   What was once regarded as
treasure, such as a talent that was in need of developing, when
realized, is often disregarded thereafter as a treasure and
becomes instead something regarded as an ability and later as
simply part of your identity.   This is what we are going to
explore in this treatise.   A treasure that you do not as yet
recognize is going to be recognized.   Once recognized it will
begin to be regarded as an ability.   And finally, through
experience, it will become your identity.   We will begin by
discussing the nature of treasure.

1.2   Treasure is most often seen in one of two ways — as
something valuable to be sought and found or as something
found that is kept secure and cherished.

1.3   Treasure in the first sense is, first and foremost,
something that you believe exists and have defined as being of
value.   As this treatise is not concerned with material treasure,
we will not explore the dimensions of physical treasure except
to say that the feelings that cause one to think that any physical
thing is capable of being a treasure, or being treasured, are of
the ego.   We will instead assume that you have moved beyond
these ego concerns and explore the realm of internal treasures.

1.4   Those of you who have moved beyond the realm of the
ego, in your fear of returning to it, often turn away from
internal treasures that you believe, when realized, might feed

the ego. Despite many observations within this Course regarding desire, you may still fear your desire. Despite many exhortations that your purpose here is to be who you are, you may have determined that exploring your internal treasure is now unnecessary. You may well be feeling a sense of relief in having learned that who you are right now is a being of perfection, and you may find in this a somewhat peaceful resting place to dwell in for a time. You may find that despite having learned much about the need to leave judgment behind, you judge your desire to be other than you are now, including any desires related to those internal treasures you once hoped to have become abilities. You think this willingness to accept who you are now is what this course has led you to and evidence of your accomplishment. You may view this as license to stay as you are and to cease striving for more.

1.5   This resting place is indeed hallowed ground and an earned respite, a demarcation even between the old way and the new way of living. But it is not the end that is sought. No matter how peaceful this place of rest may at first seem, it will soon become stagnant and unsatisfying. Left in such a place without further instruction, you would soon return to your old ideas of heaven and see peace as a state of being for those too weary to fully live. Done with the adventures of living, you would deem yourself no longer interested in the hunt for buried treasure and see it not.

1.6   This place is not life but neither is it death, for even death is not an eternal resting *place* in the sense that you have imagined it. Even rest, once truly learned, is simply rest. It is not a resting *place*, a *place* to stop along the journey of life anymore than it is a *place* at which life stops and death reigns. It is not a point at which you arrive, never to depart. Rest, when truly learned, is a state of being in which struggle has ceased and peace has triumphed over chaos, love has triumphed over fear.

1.7   You may still see but two choices: peace or struggle. But with such an attitude, you would soon be struggling to maintain your peace. There is another choice, and it lies within.

1.8   The treasure that lies within that you do not yet fully recognize is that of unity. As you have learned much of unity within the context of this course, unity, like rest, may have come to be viewed as a place at which you can arrive. Like peace, it may feel like a bubble of protection, something that sets you apart from life and the chaos that seems to reign there. You must realize that you think in terms of "place" because you think in terms of "form." Even I have often used the idea of place as a teaching aid. But you are ready now to begin to think without the need for form.

1.9   Even the desires you may have once identified as hoping to develop into abilities, are given a structure and form in your thinking of them. A desire to paint, in your thoughts becomes a completed painting that you hang upon your wall. The time of painting becomes a place. A room or studio is envisioned in which all the tools of the artist's trade are available. An aspiring pianist imagines a grand piano and performances in a magnificent concert hall or a little spinet that will grace a living room and invite friends and family to gather round. A writer sees a book in print, a runner wins a race, a tennis player becomes a champion. These are all scenes of things and places, or in other words, of the external, of form.

1.10   Thinking without form is a harbinger of unity. Form is a product of the separation. Thought "forms" are the product of the separation. Unity is not a place or a thing but the realm of the one heart and one mind: the realm of the formless and timeless, but also the realm of connectedness, of what binds all that lives in creation with the Creator.

1.11　You are the creator, but a creator who creates with thought unlike to any thoughts you have had before. Your thoughts of a grand piano will never create a grand piano. What kind of thoughts, then, would create a pianist?

1.12　Thoughts joined in unity. Thoughts joined in unity can be likened to thinking without thought. They can be likened to imagination. They can be likened to love.

1.13　Ego desires cause one to think of a grand piano. Thoughts joined in unity hear music. Ego desires cause one to think of an elaborately framed painting. Thoughts joined in unity see beauty. You are used to thinking that if you do not have a tangible goal, such as that of music lessons or the purchase of a piano, you will never reach the goals associated with those tangible steps. Thoughts joined in unity create without goals or planning, without effort or struggle. This does not make an instrument unnecessary for a musician or mean that a painter will not eventually put a brush to a canvas, but it does mean that the treasure exists without these "things" and that the treasure is already a fully realized creation. The treasure already *is* and it is already valuable and available.

1.14　This is a first step in the change in thinking that needs to occur. It is an elementary step and one easily accomplished with but a bit of willingness. This change in thinking in regards to treasures you do recognize will pave the way for recognition of treasures you heretofore have not recognized.

chapter 2

To Hear the Call

2.1   Why would we begin a Treatise on Unity by talking of treasure? To pave the way for talking of calling. What is it in you that recognizes talents that lie fully realized within? The practical mind is not the source of such imagination. The practical mind makes of imagination a fantasy. It is the heart that sees with true imagination, the heart that speaks to you in terms that are consistent with the idea you currently hold of hearing a call or having a calling.

2.2   Having a calling is spoken of in lofty terms. Few outside of those who feel they have a calling for something beyond their ordinary, limited, view of the themselves use this phrase. But many recognize that they have a calling even unto things the world considers mundane.

2.3   How does a farmer explain that she or he cannot be other than a farmer? Rising and setting with the sun is in their blood, in the very nature of who they are. Being one with the land is essential to them.

2.4   What bravery it takes in today's world to follow a calling to teach. To set aside other careers that offer far more prestige and economic gain to instead be a sharer of knowledge, a shaper of minds.

2.5   What overriding kindness calls one to take care of another's body, to be a healer?

2.6   How does one explain a joy that is like no other and that comes from the simple act of caring for a child, preparing a meal, bringing grace and order to a home?

2.7   This list of different callings could be endless, and each could be considered unexplainable.   Those who seek an explanation before following a calling, who look for reasons of a practical nature, who would seek guarantees of the rightness and outcome of following such a call, seek for proof they have already been given.   The call itself is proof.   It is proof of the heart's ability to be heard.   Of the heart's ability to recognize the unseen and to imagine the existence of that which will reveal its true nature and its joy.

2.8   All of you are capable of hearing the truth of what the heart would tell you.   You are just as capable of believing in that truth as of doubting it.   All that prevents you from believing in truth is a mind and heart acting in separation rather than in union.

2.9   You think that what prevents you from being who you are is far broader than this simple idea of hearing and following a calling would indicate.   You think what prevents you from being who you are is far broader than a division between mind and heart.   Some of you would say you feel no calling or that you feel many.   Others would cite practical reasons for doing other than what they feel called to do.   All of these ideas illustrate your belief that something other than your own willingness is necessary.   Only in your own willingness does anything exist, because only in your willingness is the power of creation expressed.

chapter 3

To Answer the Call

3.1   Your life is already an act of creation. It *was* created. All of it. It exists, fully realized within you. Your work here is to express it. *You* are far more than your life here. *You* created your life here in union with the one mind and one heart, in union, in other words, with God. Everything you have ever wanted to be *is*. Everything you have ever thought or imagined *is* and is reflected in the world you see. The only difference between the life you are living and the life you want lies in your willingness to express who you are.

3.2   There would be no need for form if there had been no desire for expression. Life *is* the desire to express outwardly what exists within. What I refer to so often here as being within, as if "within" is a *place* in which something resides, is unity and it is the *place* where being resides. It is the *place* or *realm* of one heart and one mind. It is the *place* where everything already exists fully realized. It is like a trunk full of treasure. Like a menu of possibilities. All you must do is wholeheartedly recognize the treasure you have already chosen to bring to the world. Your heart speaks to you of this treasure and guides you to open the trunk and release it to the world — to your world — to the human world. In the realm of unity where your being resides this is already accomplished. Your link between the realm of unity and the realm of physicality is your heart. Your heart tells you of the *already accomplished* and bids you to express it with your physicality, thus uniting the two realms through expression.

3.3 Your mind exists in unity. Your heart exists *where you think you are*, providing the means for union between *where you think you are* and where your being actually resides. Remember always that your heart is where the Christ in you abides and that the Christ is your identity. Remember that it is the Christ in you who learns and raises learning to the holiest of levels. It is the Christ in you who learns to walk the earth as child of God, as who you really are.

3.4 This was stated early in *A Course of Love* and is returned to now for a specific reason. While the truth that it is the Christ in you who learns may have been given little attention as you began your learning, it cannot now be ignored. Now *you* have realized your learning. *You* have begun to see the changes that your learning is capable of bringing to your life. *You* have felt the peace and love of the embrace. *You* know that you are experiencing something real and learning something that is of relevance even within the daily life you currently move through. Now you must fully recognize the distinction between the ego-self that previously was the self of learning and experience, and the Christ Self that is now the Self of learning and experience. You must take on the mantle of your new identity, your new Self.

3.5 It is this recognition that you are now acting and living in the world as your Christ Self rather than as your ego-self that will aid you in expression. Without expression, the return to unity that has been accomplished will not be realized.

3.6 If you still balk at the idea that the Christ could be in need of learning, then your idea of the Christ is still based on an old way of thinking, as are your ideas of learning.

3.7 Learning and accomplishment are not linear as you have perceived them to be. If we return to the idea of talents this may be easier to explain. If the ability to create beautiful music already exists within you, you do not have to learn what beautiful music is, only how to express it. If you see beauty within, you do not have to learn what beauty is, only how to express it. Expression and creation are not synonymous. Creation is a continuous and on-going expansion of the same thought of love that brought life into existence. The seeds of creation exist in everything and provide for continuing creation. The seeds of all that you can express exist within you, in the creation that is you. The power of creation is released through your choice, your willingness to express that aspect of creation. It is quite literally true that the seeds of much of creation lie dormant within you, already accomplished but awaiting expression in this realm of physicality.

3.8   In this same way, then, Christ can be seen as the seed of your identity. Christ is the continuous and on-going expansion of the same thought of love that brought life into existence. Christ is your identity in the broadest sense imaginable. Christ is your identity within the unity that is creation.

chapter 4

the Call to Who You Are

4.1   Creation is not an aspect of this world alone. Creation is an aspect of the whole, the all of all, the alpha and the omega, eternity and infinity. It is not only life as you know it now, but life in all its aspects. It is life beyond death as well as life before birth and life during your time here. It is all one because it is all from the same Source.

4.2   You are not only *part* of creation, but as has been said many times, a creator, and as such a continuing *act* of creation. This does not mean that creation is acted out upon you but that you are acted out upon creation. The idea of creation as something static would be completely contrary to the meaning of creation. Yet you continue to think that you stand apart from it and affect it not. This is consistent to the thinking that would tell you that you are at the mercy of fate. Fate and creation are hardly the same thing. You are at the mercy only of your own ego and only until you willingly let it go.

4.3   *A Course in Miracles* and *A Course of Love* work hand-in-hand because the change of thinking taught within *A Course in Miracles* was a change of thinking about yourself. It attempted to dislodge the ego-mind that has provided you with an identity that you but *think* you are. *A Course of Love* then followed in order to reveal to you who you truly are. While you continue to act within the world as who you *think* you are rather than as who you are, you have not integrated these two pieces of learning.

4.4   This is the stage of learning that you are at and what this treatise addresses. This treatise is attempting to show you how to *live* as who you are, and how to act within the world as the new Self you have identified. Just like learning how to swim, it is a new way of movement. Just as moving through water is a way of movement quite inconsistent with that of moving on land, so too is the new way of acting out or expressing who you are quite inconsistent with the way in which you have formerly acted out or expressed who you are. This is, of course, because you formerly acted out of a set of conditions that corresponded to who you *think* you are rather than who you truly are.

4.5   You will almost literally continue to "bump into" who you think you are as you complete the process of unlearning. It might be best explained by continuing with the swimming metaphor. If acting in the world as who you truly are is like swimming, bumping into who you think you are could be likened to trying to move within water as you would on land. Why, when moving freely through the water would you suddenly try to move as if on land? The explanation could be as simple as forgetting where you are, or as complex as a sudden panic or fear brought on by any number of factors. Either way, the result would always be the same: a sudden change from ease of movement to struggle, from going with the flow to resistance.

4.6   A first step in learning to recognize when you are acting upon notions of who you think you are rather than on who you truly are, is the appearance of struggle or resistance. As a swimmer quickly learns, the only way to return to ease of movement is to cease to struggle or resist. The ability to let go of struggle is a learned ability for the swimmer, and it is a learned ability for you now as you journey back to your real Self. It requires remembrance, trust, and a wholehearted approach that allows the body, mind, and heart to act in unison. This wholehearted approach is the condition from which unity is recognized. The water is not taken for granted but always recognized as the condition of the swimmer's environment. You are no longer confined to the conditions of separation, my dear brothers and sisters, and this is what it is time for you to learn.

4.7   This applies directly to your *reaction* to all that occurs within your life. Let us look now at your reaction to the idea put forth earlier of having a calling.

4.8   Despite whatever way you currently have of identifying calling as it relates to you, there are few among you who have not reacted to the idea of calling with two sets of feelings and thoughts. One set of thoughts and feelings contain all that one might attribute to the glad acceptance of a gift of high value, or in other words, a treasure. Another set of thoughts and feelings contain all that one might attribute to the somewhat onerous onset of yet another responsibility, another obligation. One set of thoughts recognizes that something has been given. The other set recognizes that something has been asked. The wholehearted response is one that recognizes that giving and receiving are the same in truth.

4.9   While two sets of thoughts and feelings exist, the only way to come to peace with them is through an acceptance of ambiguity. While an acceptance of ambiguity might seem preferable to conflict, an acceptance of ambiguity is a rejection of your power. What is required to claim your power is the willingness to move through the conflict of two opposing sets of thoughts and feelings to the place of unity.

4.10   Thus the next steps in our work with regard to calling are recognizing the dualistic nature of your thoughts and feelings, followed by a willingness to move past both ambiguity and conflict to union.

4.11   This requires an examination of your specific notions concerning calling as you apply them to yourself. Whether you feel that you a have a specific calling, no calling, or many callings, matters not at this juncture. What matters is that you think it does. You think it matters because you compare and judge rather than accept.

4.12   You who have so recently felt the peace of true acceptance are not asked to leave that peace to go in search of calling but are rather asked to listen from within that peace to what you feel called to do. This is not about the past and all those things that at one time or another you thought would bring you fulfillment. This is about recognizing who you are *now*. This is not a quick fix that calls you to what might have been and tells you that if you had but acted earlier you would have had the life you've dreamed of and maybe it is not too late. This is not about examining where the various calls you responded to previously have led you. All these notions are concerned with who you have thought yourself to be, not with who you are. They do not recognize the difference between thinking and knowing.

4.13   Being who you are is what you are called to do. You are asked to live a life as seamless as that of the birds of the air. You are asked to live a life where there is no division between who you are and what you do. This place of no division is the place of unity.

4.14   Now you may feel as if this treatise has led around in a circle, bringing you back only to contemplate again the acceptance of where you are now. To accept where you are is not the same as accepting who you are. Accepting *where* you are, as if it is a static place at which you have arrived, is not the goal that has been set. Accepting *who* you are includes acceptance of creation. The acceptance of creation is the acceptance of change and growth but neither of these are concepts that you understand truly. Change is not negative and growth does not imply lack.

4.15   You must be beginning to see that your thought processes, the very thought processes that tell you hour-by-hour and minute-by-minute how to perceive of and live in your world, are still often based on old concepts. This does not mean you have not changed nor that you are in need of accomplishment rather than the already accomplished. What this means is that you are still in need of unlearning, of undoing old patterns of thought. This is atonement and it is continuous and ongoing until it is no longer needed. Anything continuous and ongoing is part of creation. The very act of undoing old patterns is an act of creation. As the old is undone, a vacuum is not created. The new is created.

4.16   You are in the process of unmaking what you have made. The old structure is coming down so that the new, what might be likened to a building with no frame, can rise.

4.17   This process too is union for it is giving and receiving as one although you recognize it not as such. It is not a process of waiting until one thing is accomplished for another to begin. What is happening now is happening in unison. As the old goes, the new arrives. There is no time-lapse in this learning and so it is a condition of miracle-readiness. The old is replaced by the new simultaneously.

4.18   This is why you do not have to "wait" to hear your calling even though some of you may feel as if you are in a time of waiting for you hear no such call. The call is to be who you are and this is happening at lightning speed, a speed that cannot be measured because of its simultaneous nature. As was said within *A Course of Love*, time is but a measurement of the "time" it takes for learning to occur. As this notion of time dissolves, the state of miracle-readiness becomes your natural state.

4.19   While this adjustment of your thinking may not seem to be the miracle that it truly is, as your awareness of it grows, it is going to rise to a level you will come to think of as an ability. As your old way of responding to life causes you to struggle or resist and the new way of thinking replaces that old pattern with a new pattern of response, you will begin to see that each new response is the answer to a call that your heart alone can hear. Your heart has now become your eyes and ears. Your heart hears only one call, one voice, the language of one source...that of unity.

chapter 5

the Source of Your Call

5.1   In order for you to more fully understand the life that this course calls to you, we must also talk of another aspect of being called. While we have concluded that when you listen to your heart you hear and are able to respond to the one call, this does not mean that this one call has but one request to make of you, as in a call to be a minister, nor that it will come in but one form, as in a call to action. We have talked heretofore about a calling you feel from within, as if you are listening to a new voice that reveals your talents and desires to you. This type of calling comes as a light shone into the darkness and is revelatory in nature. Other calls will come as announcements, signs, or even as seeming demands. All call you to the present where response is able to be given. All call you "back" to who you are.

5.2   Again let me stress the present-moment nature of being called. A call is, at its most basic level, a means of communication. If you are not listening, you will not hear the calls that are meant for you. If you are looking only for a specific type of call, you will miss many unlearning and learning opportunities. Thus recognition of the different calls that may now be heard is necessary.

5.3   The call that comes in the form of an announcement is the call that carries with it no ambiguity. The certainty of an announcement can alert you that it is time to act. This might be considered the highest form of call, the call from the already accomplished to the already accomplished. Such a call signals an end to learning from the lessons of the past and a beginning of learning from the new. This Course itself is such a call, an announcement of your readiness for the new. This is the all-encompassing call and is not about specifics. Because it is not about specifics you may find yourself still wondering what to do. Thus you must be aware of the calls that assist you in knowing what to do.

5.4   These calls you may think of as signs. Like literal signposts along a roadway, they alert you to turn your attention in a particular direction.

5.4   Calls that seem to come in the form of demands are often calls that come to you from within the teaching and learning ground of relationships. You may be literally "called to account" for certain attitudes or behaviors. You may also be called upon to call others to account for their attitudes or behaviors.

5.6   These last two calls, the call that appears in the form of a sign and the call that comes in the form of a demand, are about specifics in a way that the call that comes as an announcement is not. They represent the remnants of learning from the past, the final breaking of old patterns. They may seem to signal difficult times, but they are times that must be gotten through and lessons that need to be allowed to pass through you.

5.7   Until you have fully integrated the truth that giving and receiving are one, you will not fully believe that needs are not lacks. Until you have fully integrated the truth that giving and receiving are one, you will not realize that dependency is a matter of the interdependency of all that exists in relationship. All the calls that come to you in the form of signs or demands will be calls that assist you in integrating this learning and making it one with who you are. These lessons will bring who you are into focus within your mind through the vehicle of your heart.

67

chapter 6

the Belief: Accomplishment

6.1   The source of what we have been speaking of as "calling" is your heart. It is what alerts you to the treasures that lie within. There is no time in the place we are calling *within* and your heart knows not of time even while it adheres to the rules of time you would place upon yourself. Cease adhering to the rules of time and see how much more the language of your heart becomes known to you.

6.2   I speak here not of the rules of time that govern your days and years but the rules of time that you *believe* govern your days and years and that you thus allow to govern your thinking. If time is but a measure of learning and if your learning is now at the stage at which it occurs in unison with unlearning, then the end of time as you know it is close at hand. If you can begin now to think without the barriers of time you but place upon your thinking, you will advance this process and more quickly bring about the end of the pattern of learning that you refer to as time. The end of the pattern of learning that you refer to as time is the beginning of the time of unity.

6.3   This return to unity is reliant upon the changes in your beliefs that this Course has brought about. Let us review these beliefs and how they relate to your concept of time.

6.4   Only you can be accomplished and your accomplishment is already complete.

6.5   What does this mean in regard to time? You might think of being accomplished as all of your work being done. If there is no work to be done, nothing for you to do, what do you need time for? Have you ever conceived of accomplishing anything without taking into account the time that it will take? Relate this question to our discussion of treasure and you will understand what it is of which I speak. You believe that your treasures only become accomplished abilities within time. You believe that your treasures only become part of your identity when you have passed beyond the time it takes for those treasures to become abilities. Thus all that you might wish to accomplish stands separate from you and beyond you in time. That your mind projects what you desire to accomplish onto an unknown future time is what would seem to keep you from accomplishment. I say that it is what would "seem to" purposefully. If you are already accomplished, this trick of your mind has not worked. And yet if you believe that this trick of your mind has worked, you act as if you are being kept from accomplishment by time and this "seems" quite real to you. This "seems" quite real to you because of what you believe.

6.6   Accomplishment is not an end point but a given. It is not an outcome but a certainty. It says *I am* rather than *I will be*. *I will be* is a statement that presumes a future in which you will be someone other than who you are in the present. Unity exists only in the here and now of the present. There is no *will be* in unity. There is only what *is*. The limits you would place on the concept of something being what it *is*, must be part of this discussion.

6.7   Your mind would tell you that a chair is a chair and regard it as a fact. Through the learning you have done since your birth, you have come to recognize a chair as having certain properties, the most essential of which is that it is a structure on which to sit. The exercises of *A Course in Miracles* began with asking you to call into question these beliefs in known, observable, facts. You may have regarded these exercises as silly or you may have thought of the lessons of physics and felt as if you understood these exercises on an intellectual level.

But what these exercises have prepared you for is an acceptance of the ongoing change that *is* creation; an acceptance that something can be what it *is*, a known fact, an object with an identity, but also part of the ongoing nature of creation. Could this be true of a chair and not be true of you?

6.8   It is your belief that change and growth are indicative of all that *can be* accomplished rather than of what is *already* accomplished that needs adjustment now. As a tree exists fully accomplished within its seed and yet grows and changes, you exist fully accomplished within the seed that is the Christ in you even while you continue to grow and change. Physical form and action of all kinds are but expressions of that which already exist within the seed of the already accomplished.

6.9   The recognition that you are already accomplish-ed is a condition of your recognition of the state of unity. It is a recognition that you exist in unity *outside* of the pattern of time. Miracles *create* an out-of-pattern time interval. Living in a state of miracle-readiness is the creation of a new reality outside of the pattern of ordinary time. Although this state exists as the already accomplished, it is up to you to create it for yourself. You must create it for yourself only because you believe you replaced what was already accomplished with what you made. This is what is happening as you unlearn and learn in unison. You are creating the state of unity as a new reality for *your Self* even though it is actually a return to what has always been. You are changing the world you perceive by perceiving a new world. You are changing from who you have thought yourself to be to who you are.

6.10   As I have already said that your heart must exist where you think you are, you can begin to see that this change in thinking will release your heart, returning it to its natural realm. Thus does mind and heart join in unity in the present, in the here and now, so that you exist, even within form, as the only Son of God, the Christ, the word made flesh. Remember that the phrase, *the Son of God*, and the name *Christ*, but represent the original creation and are not to be mistaken for heavenly deities separate from you. The Christ is your *Self* as you were created and remain. The Christ is the accomplished Self.

chapter 7

the Belief: Giving and Receiving As One

7.1   We have talked much in this course of your desire to be independent without looking at the condition of dependency that you consider its opposite. To be independent, you feel as if you must rely only on your self. The connotation of reliance on others, or dependence, has taken on a negative meaning specifically in contrast to your desire to be independent. One of your greatest fears is of a condition that causes you to be dependent or to rely on others.

7.2   "Others" are the great unknown of living in the world. "Others" are those who are beyond your control, those who can influence the course of your day or your life in ways you would not choose. "Others" represent the accidents waiting to happen, love that is not returned, the withholding of things you deem important. This fear that you feel in relation to others is as true of those you hold most dear to you as it is of those you would call strangers. It is the very independence of others that makes your own independence seem so important to you. Dependency is not consistent with your notions of a healthy self. What, then is the alternative?

7.3   The alternative is believing in giving and receiving as one.

7.4   First let us replace your idea of others with the idea of relationship that has been so often defined and repeated within this course. In order to believe in giving and receiving as one, you must believe in relationship rather than in others.

7.5   Those you would view as others are separate from you. Those you would view as being in relationship with you are not separate from you. The relationship is the source of your unity. That you exist in relationship with all is a belief that you must now incorporate into living. Further, you must remember that relationship is based on trust.   If you are dependent, or supported by others with whom you share a trusting relationship, where is the negativity?   Where is the cause for fear?   What is the hidden source of your feelings of lack or deprivation?   What is the hidden source of your desire to control?

7.6   This source is the ego. Even now, the ego will take every opportunity that arises to prove to you that independence is a far better state than that of dependence.   It will work diligently to convince you that any course that tries to take away your independence should be resisted. As long as you continue to listen to your ego you will not understand giving and receiving as one and will not believe in it.

7.7   This is the most difficult belief of all to integrate into the living of your life. Each time another thwarts you, you will be tempted to believe that giving and receiving as one is not taking place. Your previous pattern of behavior will be quick to assert itself and you will feel resentment and claim that the situation is unfair. You will be tempted to withhold as "others" withhold from you.

7.8   Is it not clear how important it is to living in peace that this pattern be broken? Will you live in peace only until some "other" breaks your peace?   Only until some circumstance beyond your control brings an unexpected conflict your way?

7.9   There is no function for control in unity. There is no need for it. Relationship is the only means through which interaction is real, the only source of your ability to change that which you would change.

7.10   Here is an idea not heretofore given much attention, the idea of the desire for change. Certainly there will continue to be things within your life that are in need of change. As was stated in the beginning of this treatise, this course has not called you to a static state of sameness, an acceptance of who you are that does not allow for change. But once you have become happier with who you are, you will, if left un-schooled, turn your attention to others and to situations you would have be different than they are. You will want to be a change-agent. You will want to move into the world and be an active force within it. This is an aim consistent with the teachings of this course, but what will prevent you from following the patterns of old as you go out into the world with your desire to effect change?

7.11   The only thing that will prevent this is your ability to go out into the world and remain who you are. This relates to giving and receiving being one in truth in a very concrete way. For to go out into the world with the desire to give, either expecting to receive in certain measure or to receive not at all, is to follow the old pattern, a pattern that has been proven to not have any ability to change the world.

7.12   To proceed into each relationship as who you truly are, is to bring everlasting change to each and every relationship, and thus to all.

7.13   Again I return you to the early teachings of *A Course of Love,* teachings concerning your desire to be good and to do good. This is not about doing good works. This is about being who you are and seeing the truth rather than the illusion that surrounds you. You cannot, in other words, be a good person in a bad world. You cannot affect change without, without having affected change within. You cannot be independent and still be of service. For as long as you believe in your independence you will not accept your dependence. You will not accept giving and receiving as one if you feel able only to give or as if "others" have nothing you would receive.

7.14 This new attitude, then, includes accepting that you have needs. Saying that you are a being who exists in relationship is the same as saying you are a being who needs relationships. The only thing in this new pattern that keeps you from being needy and dependent in an unhealthy way, is that you believe in giving and receiving as one. You believe, in other words, that your needs will be provided for, thus ceasing to be needs. To deny that you are a being with needs is not the aim of this course. To come to believe that your needs are provided for by a Creator and a creation that includes all "others" is to believe in giving and receiving being one in truth.

7.15 Giving is not only about choosing what good and helpful parts of yourself you will share with the world. It is also about giving the world the opportunity to give back. It is about recognizing the constant and ongoing exchange that allows needs to be met. It is trusting that if you have a need for money, or time, or honesty, or love, it will be provided.

7.16 Trusting is not a condition or state of being that you have heretofore seen as being an active one. Your attitude toward trust is one of waiting, as if an active stance toward trust would be *dis*trustful. You will often say that you trust when what you are doing is hoping for a specific outcome. Real trust is not a trust that waits and hopes but a trust that acts from who you truly are. Real trust requires the discipline of being who you are in every circumstance and in every relationship. Real trust begins with your Self.

7.17 How often have you hidden thoughts and feelings because you question whether they are legitimate thoughts and feelings? For some of you this answer has changed greatly over time. But for many of you, you have become less, rather than more forthcoming about your thoughts and feelings since taking this Course. You have done so out of a desire to be truthful, a desire to not express thoughts and feelings unworthy of your real Self. You may have increasingly denied thoughts and feelings you would judge as negative or bad. Or you may have, in your desire not to judge others, kept yourself from speaking up in instances where you previously would have stated an opinion. While these modes of behavior, in themselves, are learning aides that prepare you for acting with the certainty you seek, they again are not to be confused with the true aims of this course of study.

7.18   Who you are cannot be denied in favor of who you "will be." Needs cannot be denied as a means of having them cease to be. You who are beginning to realize that you have much to give, realize that you have as much to receive and that receiving does not imply that you are lacking!

7.19   The discipline required to be who you are is a discipline that requires trust in self and honesty in relationships. Does this mean that you are required to express every thought and feeling that comes your way? No, but this does mean that you bring the thoughts and feelings that arise to the place within your heart that has been prepared for them. You do not deny them. You bring them first to your Self, to the Self joined in unity at the place of your heart. From this place you learn to discriminate, to separate the false from the true, for your ego thoughts cannot long abide in the holy place of your heart. With truth and illusion separated, you develop the discipline to express your true Self, as you are now. This is the only way the Self you are now has to grow and change. This is the only means the Self you are now has of giving and receiving as one. This is the only means available to you to replace the old pattern with the new.

7.20   The recognition that giving and receiving occur as one is a precondition for your recognition of the state of unity. As with the recognition of your accomplishment, the acceptance of the belief that giving and receiving are one in truth changes the function of time as you know it. There is not a period of waiting or a period of time between giving and receiving. There is not a time lapse between the recognition of needs and the meeting of needs. It is accepted that giving and receiving occur in unison, thus further collapsing the need for time.

7.21   While, as stated previously, this belief will at times seem difficult to put into practice, and while your recognition of receiving and of needs being met may seem to still take time, this belief builds on that of the already accomplished through experience. As you *experience* giving and receiving being one your belief will become true conviction. Your ability to recognize giving and receiving as one becomes an aspect of your identity and is accepted as the nature of who you are in truth.

chapter 8

the Belief: No Relationships are Special

8.1   In order for this learning to come to completion, you must put into practice the belief that no relationships are special. Your loyalty must be totally to the truth of who you are and not continue to be split by special relationships. While your love relationships will provide a rich learning ground for you now, they must also now be separated from all that would continue to make them special.

8.2   The one you come to know through relationship is your Self. This is the learning ground on which you now stand. All that prevents you from being who are within your relationships must be let go.   All that will complement who you are must be received.   Thus the nature of many relationships may be required to change. Remember that there is no loss but only gain or you will feel threatened by what you will imagine to be loss.   Remember too the practice of devotion spoken of within the Course, for in this practice is the truth separated from illusion.

8.3   While your dedication to the goal of being who you are may at first seem selfish, it will soon be revealed to be the most sincere form of relationship. Relationship based on anything other than who you are is but a mockery of relationship. The calls that come to you now as signs and demands will not only aid you in your realization of who you are and your ability to live as who you are, but will aid all others. This is giving and receiving as one. What you gain will take nothing from anyone.

What another is able to give you will take nothing from them, and what you are able to give another will take nothing from you.

8.4   These are all calls to know your Self and to act on this knowing. These are calls to truth and but take the form of honesty for a brief time as the truth of who you are is revealed to you and through your relationships to all.

8.5   A new type of acceptance is required here, one not previously asked or expected of you. This is an acceptance that you know your own truth and an acceptance that your truth will not change. As we have said that you are not called to a static acceptance that does not include change, this new idea of acceptance requires further clarification.

8.6   It was said often within *A Course of Love* that the truth does not change. The truth of who you are has not changed and you are as you were created. Form and behavior are, however, subject to change, as are your expressions of who you are. This distinction must be fully realized here in order for you to accept the truth of who you are and to come to an acceptance of the unchangeable nature of this truth. This is akin to being done with seeking. This is the final acceptance that you have "found" and that you have been found. You need no longer journey onto the paths of seeking. The truth of yourself that you reveal now will not become a new truth as you take a new path. Your path now is sure and its final acceptance necessary. You are the prodigal sons and daughters who have returned home. Your stay is not finite. You are not here to rest and gain strength for another journey in search of something that is not available here. Here is the realm of the already accomplished. This is home. Your expression of who you are may lead you to many new adventures but never again to the special relationships that would take you away from your true Self. Never again will you be away from home for home is who you are, a "place" you carry within you, a place that is you. This is the home of unity.

8.7   How much time will be saved by an end to empty seeking? You have already arrived and need no time to journey any longer. How much time will be saved by an end to the maintenance required by special relationships? When all relationships are holy, you have no need to maintain special-ness.

8.8   Thus again is your learning advanced by leaps and bounds formerly reserved for the angels. You are your own wings, your relationships but the breeze that keeps you afloat.

Chapter 9
the Belief: No Loss but only Gain

9.1   I ask you now to remember a time when you felt from another the desire to help or to meet your needs. Do not think that this desire is not present in all relationships. It is only the ego that stands between desire and the meeting of desire, needs and the meeting of needs.

9.2   The word *need* and the word *dependent* are only words and words that would be inconceivable to you in the state of unity before you left it. Now, they are just tools, as are many other means of practice that assist you in bypassing your ego mind. Some practices more commonly thought of as tools might be meditation, exercises of the body such as yoga, or exercises of the mind such as affirmations. These tools are all means of releasing the ego mind and inviting the one mind, or unity, into the present moment. When seen as such, all these tools, including needs, can ignite the combination of learning and unlearning, the letting go of one so that the other can arrive.

9.3   We are now beginning to speak of the second aspect of treasure that was addressed in the beginning of this treatise as something found that is kept secure and cherished. This aspect of treasure relates to your ability to let go. As many of you will find the idea of letting go of special relationships among the most difficult of ideas contained in this course of study, the ability to let go must be further discussed.

When a need is fulfilled, you have been accustomed to having a reaction to this meeting of a need as if it takes place apart from you, or from outside of you. You assign the meeting of a need to a person or system or organization. You as often feel indebted as you feel grateful for the meeting of needs. When your life is running smoothly and needs are being continuously met, you begin to want to hang on to the relationships that you feel met these needs *because* of their ability to meet them. When your needs cease being met, you believe there has been a loss such as with the loss of a job or loved one or even of the promise of some service. When you think in such a way you believe in loss rather than in the replacement belief that there is no loss but only gain.

9.5   It is perhaps best seen in the contrast implied by the intent to hang on. The desire to hang on to anything assumes that what you have is in need of protection or that it would not be secure without your effort to keep it secure. Inherent in this assumption is the concept of "having" or ownership. How does this relate to "having" needs? By identifying needs in such a way, in the same way that you identify "having" in regards to possessions, you but continue to feel as if you "have" needs even long after they have been met. Since I have already stated that you do have needs this may seem confusing.

9.6   In relationship, every need is met by a corresponding need. It is a dance of correspondence.

9.7   All needs are shared. This is what differentiates needs from wants. This is true in two senses. It is true in that all needs, from survival needs to needs for love are literally shared in the same measure by all. The other sense in which needs are shared is in the aspect of correspondence. They are shared because they are known. Every being inherently knows that it shares the same needs as every other being of its kind. Every being also inherently knows that needs and the fulfillment of needs are part of the same fabric — they are like puzzle pieces that fit together. Other beings that share life with you on this planet are not concerned with needs or need fulfillment. Doing what needs to be done in order to survive is hardly the same as feeling that one has a need. Needs are the domain of the thinking being only. Thinking beings share needs because of the way in which they think. That some seem to have more needs than others is a fallacy of perception. Not one has more needs than another.

9.8   What is shared by all is not owned. What all have is in no danger of being taken away. All that you are capable of having you already have as the already accomplished. All that you would give will take nothing away from you.

9.9   This could be restated as the belief that there is no loss but only gain.

9.10   The extent to which you deny your needs or are honest about your needs makes the difference in your connection or separation within relationship. The extent to which you are willing to abdicate your needs in order to attain something is the extent to which your belief in want or lack is revealed. This is the purview of special relationships. The very compromises you are often prone to make in special relationships are but the symptoms of your fear.

9.11   As soon as you are content or self-satisfied, or, in other words, feel your needs are met, the desire to hang on to what you have arises. This is true of knowledge, or what you know, and of who you are, just as much as it is of special relationships and what you might more readily think of as treasure, such as a successful career or inspired creative project.

9.12   As soon as the desire to hang on arises, both learning and unlearning cease to occur. The desire to maintain a state you believe you have achieved and have labeled a state in which your needs are met creates a static level, that no matter how good or right or meaningful, loses its creative nature by remaining static.

9.13   So how do you remain within the constant creative flux or flow of creation without either constantly striving for more of what you already have or for what you consider progress? You need a means of disconnecting this drive that has become instinctual to you. As a being existing in form, you have honed certain instincts over millennia, such as the instinct to survive, in order to carry on in physical form.

9.14   There is no such thing as a static level in unity where creation is continuous and ongoing. You should have no desire to reach such a state and the awareness that you are in such a state can alert you, or serve as a sign, that the ego-mind and its fear-based thinking has momentarily returned. This does not mean that you will never be at rest or that you will be constantly seeking to arrive. As has already been said, you have arrived and rest exists only in the state of unity.

9.15   Because you have not thought previously of needs as tools every bit as valuable as the others mentioned here, this adjustment in your thinking may seem difficult to accept. How does the identification of needs or the dependency inherent in relationships by-pass the ego-mind? They heretofore have not, only because of your perception of them as signals of what you are lacking. Once this perception has shifted, you ego-mind will cease to be fed by these concerns. What is food for the ego-mind is fear and the removal of these final fears will quite literally starve the ego-mind out of existence.

9.16   An understanding of the mutuality of needs will aid you in being honest about your needs, thus allowing them to be met. Then the need to define or to identify them ceases. Your needs only continue to be brought to your awareness as needs until your trust in their immediate and ongoing fulfillment is complete. Once this trust is realized you will no longer think in terms of needs at all. Once you are no longer concerned with needs and the meeting of needs you will no longer be concerned with special relationships. You will realize that there is no loss but only gain involved in letting them go.

9.17   Holding on to what you think will meet your needs is like holding your breath. Your breath cannot long be held. It is only through the inhaling and exhaling, the give and take of breathing that you live. Each time you are tempted to think that your needs can only be met in special ways by special relationships, remember this example of holding your breath. Think in such a way no longer than you can comfortably hold your breath. Release your breath and release this fear and move from special to holy relationship.

9.18   This phase of coming to accept need and dependency is necessary only as a learning ground of experience on which trust can grow. Once this trust is realized you will no longer think of trust just as you will no longer think of needs.

9.19   Ceasing to think in these terms will soon be seen as a valuable ability and a timesaving measure of great magnitude. As these old ways of thinking leave you, you will be left as who you are in truth.

chapter 10

the Belief: We Only Learn in Unity

10.1   You would have to work mightily to turn the lessons of this course into a tool, but many of you will not tire of this work until you succeed. This is how truths become dogma and dogma becomes tyranny. This happens by accepting a static state. A static state is not a living state because creation is not occurring within it. This is a living course. This is why you are called to live it rather than to take it. This is why you are called to be a teacher and a learner both. This is how the exchange of giving and receiving as one occurs. This exchange *is* unity.

10.2   Thinking that needs can be met only in certain ways is akin to another belief that has been replaced. This belief was first expressed in *A Course in Miracles* by the saying *Resign as your own teacher*. This belief in the self as teacher has now been replaced with the belief that you only learn in unity.

10.3   I ask you to think for a moment of a time when you attempted to recall a specific memory. This may have been a memory of a name or address, of a dream, or an attempt to recall a specific event. At such times, you often feel as if, just as the memory is about to return to you, it is swatted away as easily and routinely as a hand swats away a fly. You know that the information is contained within you and still you are often forced to accept an inability to have access to this information. It is forced from your awareness by something you know not. It is there and yet swatted away as if by some unseen hand. Where has this information gone and what keeps it from you? You might feel frustrated with your memory at such a time and even say something such as "my brain just isn't working right today." I want you now to keep this example in mind as we explore learning in unity.

10.4   You might think of unity as you have so often thought of your brain, but rather than thinking of it in the singular, think of it as a storehouse or giant brain in which all that has ever been known or thought is contained. The technology that has created super-computers will immediately come to mind from this illustration. While this illustration may be distasteful to some and intriguing to others, how many of you would not want to replace your ability to know with the ability of a super-computer?

10.5   While just an illustration, the reverse of this is akin to what you have done by replacing unity with singularity. You have narrowed your ability to know to an ability to know that which you have experienced. While what we are speaking of as knowing has little to do with the information stored in super-computers, it is still a worthy illustration. For just as a super-computer needs a knowledgeable operator in order to provide the information sought, so too do you need to become knowledgeable in order to access all that is available to you.

10.6   Just as needs have been shown to be shared in like measure by all, so too is true knowing. Just as needs were shown to be distinguishable from wants by a discussion of their shared nature, so too now must knowing be distinguished from what you consider intelligence.

10.7   While you are being told that you can no longer believe that what you know is related to experience, you are not being told that you have exactly the same knowledge as does every person of every variety and level of experience. Yet no one can know more of the truth than another, and no one can know less.

10.8   Just beyond your mind's ability to call it forth lies the truth that you and all other beings know. The access to what seems to lie beyond your ability lies in the Christ in you. You might think of the ego as the hand that swats away this knowing.

10.9   The ego is the teacher you have relied upon when you have relied upon your self as your own teacher.

10.10   You forget constantly that the Christ in you is the learner here. What need is there for a computer brain or for the ego to be your teacher when the learner in you is the all-powerful? The learner in you is the unifying force of the universe. The learning you are in need of is the learning that will call who you are back to your united mind and heart. This is the knowing that already exists, the memory that is swatted away by the ego.

10.11   Why, then, is this called learning? Learning simply means to come to know. If what you know has been forgotten, you still are in need of the learning that assists you in coming to know once again.

10.12   But as long as you continue to attempt to learn with your ego, or in other words, as long as you would continue to attempt to learn in the same way that you have previously learned, you will not learn because the "you" that will be involved in the learning process will not be the real you.

10.13   The Christ in you is the real you. The Christ in you is the Self you become when you have united heart and mind once again in wholeheartedness. The union of mind and heart is the first union, the union that must precede all the rest. You are in a state of unity when you have achieved wholeheartedness. You are in a state in which you are able to learn. I am here to show you the way to the Christ in you. I began my teaching by appealing to your heart so as to ready you for the return of wholeheartedness, the state of union in which all that you learn is shared, first by mind and heart, and then in unity with your brothers and sisters. You achieve this state only by listening to one voice, or, in other words, by ending the separated state which is the state in which the ego exists. The end of the separated state or the ego, is the beginning of your ability to hear only one voice, the voice we all share in unity.

10.14 This voice speaks to you in a thousand ways. It is the voice of love, the voice of creation, the voice of life. It is the voice of certainty that allows you to move through each day and all the experiences within it as who you are in truth. It releases you from the feeling of needing to control or protect your treasure. It releases you as well from the static state of trying to hang on to who you were yesterday, or trying to prevent change tomorrow.

10.15 As was said in the beginning, it is realized that it is hard for you to believe that the Christ in you is in need of learning. Think a moment of why this should be so. Is there ever a moment in which coming to know is not appropriate? Is there any reason that coming to know should not be seen as something continuous and ongoing?

10.16 Again your desire for a static state would make you rather listen to your ego as it prescribes learning for certain circumstances that would be quickly put behind you or chosen for specific outcomes. While many love to learn for the sake of learning alone, still they would be loath to give up or let go the ability to choose their lessons. And still we are only talking about learning as you have perceived of it rather than learning from life.

10.17 What difference does it make to your concepts of learning when you think of life as your course work? Would you be any more willing to let another choose your lessons for you?

10.18   What are your plans and dreams but chosen lessons? While you do not think of them as such you do not think of life as your learning ground.   You still think of lessons as being about specific subject matter.   When life does not go as you have planned, you feel as if your chosen path has been denied to you.   You often feel a sense of loss and rarely one of gain. Unless life goes the way you have intended for it to go, you do not feel gifted or blessed, not even when you may have looked back on other situations that did not go as you had planned and seen that they nevertheless gifted you with experiences or opportunities that would not have arisen had your chosen plan come to fruition.

10.19   The Christ in you has no need to plan.   A need to come to know...yes.   But a need to plan...no.   The Christ in you needs not for you to choose a lesson plan, but to let life itself be your chosen way of learning.

chapter 11

the Belief: We Exist in Relationship & Unity

11.1   The Christ in you *is* relationship. As you were told within the pages of this course, you are a being who exists *in* relationship.   This is how you were created and how you remain. This is the truth of who you are and even, in your own terms, a fact of your existence. Earlier this was pointed out to you so that you would come to accept who you are and so that you would extend forgiveness to yourself and all you hold responsible for this truth. This forgiveness has now extended in two distinct ways.   First in forgiving your Creator for creating you in such a way, and second in forgiving a world that has taught you to want to be other than who you are. Now our aim is to show you how to integrate the belief that you are a being who exists in relationship into the living of your life.

11.2   Even though you no longer want to be other than who you are, and even though you now have a much clearer understanding of who you are, you will find living as who you are in the world difficult as long as you perceive others as living under the old rules: the laws of man rather than the laws of God or love.   It will seem all but impossible to live in relationship when those around you are still convinced of their separation and still seeking to glorify it. You will still perceive the world as operating under the laws of man and as long as you perceive the world in such a way, you will be forced to live by its laws. This will cause struggle, and as you now know that struggle of any kind alerts you to the presence of ego, you will continue to do battle with the ego rather than leaving it forever behind.

11.3   Doing battle with the ego has become the pre-occupation of many gifted and learned people. This is the classic battle revealed in all myths and tales of war and strife. It is the battle that in your imaginings has extended even to the angels. The ego is the dragon that must be slain, the evil of the despot to be toppled, the one-on-one conflict of all heroes who would take sides and do battle.

11.4   You are called to peace, a peace that begins and ends with ceasing to do battle with the ego. As the ego has been the known identity of your existence until now, it will, in a sense, be forever with you, much as the body that is your form will remain with you until your death. But while your perception of your body as your identity and your home has given way to an idea of it as a form that can be of service to you and your expression, there is no service the ego can do you. The ego is the one untruth, given many names and many faces and the only thing given by you the power to do battle with the truth, or with God. Remember now and always that you and God are one and that what you invite to do battle with God you but battle yourself.

11.5   A God of love does not do battle, for truth needs no protection. The truth is not threatened by untruth. The truth simply exists, as love exists, and as you exist. When we say something *is* this is of what we speak. When we say all truth is generalizable, all needs are shared, all knowing is shared, this is of what we speak.

11.6   All cannot be threatened by nothing.

11.7   This is why we spent a fair amount of time addressing needs in a way we had not previously addressed them. Only with your understanding that all that is real is shared does the ego lose its power. The ego was made from the belief in separation and all that followed from it. Your true identity must be re-created from the belief in unity that is inherent in the acceptance that you exist in relationship. Separation is all that opposes relationship, and the ego is all that opposes your true identity.

11.8   The ego, having been with you from your earliest remembering, will continue to be with you in the way that all learned behaviors and ideas are with you, until it is totally replaced by new learning. Your new learning must complement your new beliefs. The ultimate goal of this learning is the end of the need for beliefs at all.

11.9   This learning, then, must be seen for what it is. It is the holiest of work and the final evidence of means and end being the same.   Your devotion to this learning must now be complete, your willingness total, your way of learning that of a mind and heart joined in wholeheartedness.

11.10   Realize that when you think that this total reversal of thought concerning your self and your world will be difficult you are listening to your ego. The Christ in you knows not of difficulty.

11.11   How can it be that we speak both of the Christ *in* you and of Christ as being relationship itself? How can it be that we have spoken of Christ being both wholly human and wholly divine?   These statements can only be true if there is no division between you and relationship, if there is no division between the human and the divine.

11.12   Separate things must still exist in relationship. This is the key to understanding the truth of these statements. For even while you have chosen separation, this choice did not preclude the existence of relationship and it is in relationship that union still exists.   If you had been able to choose separation without relationship, then the image of yourself the ego has put forth would have been a true image. But as life cannot exist apart from relationship, this choice was not available and did not overturn the laws of God. The ego is but your belief that this has occurred; that what could never be true has become the truth.

11.13   So let us now, for the sake of continued learning, speak of separation in a new way. Let us speak of separation as a state that exists rather than as a state that does not exist. If you exist as a separate being but your being is contingent upon relationship for its existence, is this not the same as saying that you are a being who exists in relationship? Is this not similar to saying that a living human body does not exist without its heart? Is not what is essential to a living body a fact of that body's existence? While this illustration is not attempting to say that life does not exist apart from the body, it is attempting to reveal, in an easily understandable way, that there is a condition under which you are here and able to experience life as a separate being. That condition is relationship and relationship is what keeps you forever one with your Creator.

11.14   Here that relationship is being called Christ in order to keep the holiness and importance of this relationship forever and foremost in your mind. Here, that relationship has been given a name, as we have given your relationship with your separate identity the name of ego. Here, we are asking you to choose the one real relationship and to vanquish the one unreal relationship.

11.15   It is from these two separate ideas of relationship that the concept of doing battle has emerged. This concept of doing battle can only remain if you remain convinced that the ego is real. As long as you believe that the ego is real, you will feel as if there are two identities that exist within you and you will see yourself as doing battle in countless ways and forms. There will never actually be a battle going on between Christ and the ego, but you will perceive that such battles exist. You will be prone to calling upon the Christ as your higher self to defend you against the ego self. This is highly akin to your former notion of prayer and assumes that there is something real that you need defense against or saving from. This is how the notion of Christ as savior arose. This is the belief in a good self and a bad self with Christ acting as conscience and defender of good and the ego acting as devil and defender of evil. This is nonsense, or but a form of the insanity that is prevalent still, even in your thinking. You do not realize that this source of conflict is the source of all conflict that seems real to you within your world. This battle of good and evil, while you believe in it still, will be demonstrated before you just as it has been from time immemorial. Is this what you would have continue? Does this not but reveal to you a fraction of the power of your thinking and its ability to shape the world you see?

11.16   An alternative to this insanity exists. The alternative is removing all faith from your belief in the ego self. The alternative is replacing belief in an ego self with belief in a Christ self. Total replacement. As long as you hang on to both identities the world will not change and you will not know who you are. You may think you know, and you may waste much time in perceived battles, valiantly fighting for good to win out over evil. But this is not the new way and the lack of value from this type of effort can surely now be seen.

11.17   I have said that the ego will remain with you as the identity you have learned since birth until you replace it with new learning. While you have learned much here, you may be thinking that your ego is still very much with you, and wondering, if you have not yet replaced it, how this miracle will come about. This replacement is indeed a miracle and the very miracle you have been prepared for within this course of learning.

chapter 12

the Belief: Correction and Atonement

12.1 Miracles are thoughts and I am the corrector of false thinking. You have been made ready for this correction and your belief in correction, or atonement, is the final belief that must be put into practice.

12.2 Miracles are a service provided through love. Your readiness for miracles has been achieved through the learning you have accomplished. Miracles cannot be used, and so your learning needed to include an ability to distinguish between service and use. Service, or devotion, leads to harmony through right action. Until you were able to distinguish the false from the true, you were not able to receive the power of miracles.

12.3 The power of miracles is but the culmination and the integration of the beliefs we have put forth here. The miracle I am offering you here is the service I offer you, the precursor of the service you will offer to others.

12.4 Miracles are intercessions. As such they are agreements. They do not take away free will but free the will to respond to truth. They are the ultimate acceptance of giving and receiving being one in truth.

12.5 While you continue to feel as if you do not understand miracles, you will be reluctant to believe in them or to see yourself as a miracle worker. Your belief in miracles and your belief in atonement or correction are the same. When you believe there is anything other than your own thinking that is in need of correction you think falsely. Right-thinking is the realm of miracles.

12.6 As with the learning goal being set here of going beyond belief to simply knowing, the learning goal in relation to the miracle is the same — it is one of going beyond belief in the miracle to simply knowing. Knowing is knowing the truth. Knowing is right-thinking. Your return to knowing or right-thinking is both the miracle and the end for the need of miracles. As you live in the world as who you are, you become a miracle and the constant expression of the miracle.

12.7 The power of thought and the power of prayer, once aligned, call constantly upon the same power of intercession that is the miracle. This is why we also devoted a fair amount of this treatise to a discussion of calling. Calling is not only something you receive but something you must learn to give. As you have come to see calling as a gift and a treasure as well as a learning device, so you must come to see your own ability to call forth intercession as a gift and treasure you are able to give in service to your brothers and sisters.

12.8 If callings come to alert you to the treasure within, how can it be that you, as a miracle-minded being, are not called upon to also call forth the treasure that exists around you? When you call to those whom you meet in relationship, you call but to the already accomplished.

12.9 There, between you and the "other" whom you have previously only perceived, is the relationship and the miracle waiting to happen. As we spoke within *A Course of Love* of relationship being not one thing or another but a third something, this is what we speak of here again. If Christ *is* relationship, and if the Christ *in* you is the real you, then this all-encompassing relationship, both within you and without

you, both you and all you are in relationship with, is that third
something that is the holy relationship.

12.10   This holy relationship is what you are called to cultivate
as a gardener cultivates her garden. The gardener knows that
although the plant exists fully realized within its seed, it also
needs the relationship of earth and water, light and air. The
gardener knows that tending the garden will help it to flourish
and show its abundance. The gardener knows she is part of the
relationship that is the garden. A true gardener believes not in
bad seeds. A true gardener believes not that she is in control.
A true gardener accepts the grandeur that is the garden and
finds it beautiful to behold.

12.11   This metaphor is akin to acceptance of the holy
relationship. It is acceptance of what occurs with the joining of
many factors, one no more important than another. While the
Christ in you has been compared to the seed of all you are,
what you have had revealed to you here is that the Christ is also
the relationship of all that would bring the seed to fruition.
The ego could be here compared to a gardener who believes
that the seed alone is all that is important. As intently as this
gardener might struggle to cause the seed to grow, without the
relationship of earth and water, light and air, the seed would but
remain a source of struggle. The ego would hang on to what is
already there within you, and never let you express, through
relationship, all that you are. As valuable as the ego would tell
you that you are, it still would thwart you from being who you
are through its denial of the relationships essential to that which
you truly are.

12.12   This cultivation then, of the all-encompassing holy
relationship that exists within you and without you, both in all
you are and all you are in relationship with, is how you are
called to live your life and the call you are asked to sound to all
your brothers and sisters.

12.13   Let the beliefs we have set forth become one with you so that they enable you to live and express and act as who you are in every moment and in every circumstance.   Let these abilities serve you and your brothers and sisters.   Let this way of living be the expression of who you are and all that you now remember.   Let this remembrance grow and flourish as the garden that is you.

12.14   Recognize now that unity is within you and without you, in all you are and in all with whom you are in relationship. Feel the embrace and the love that is this unity and know that it is you, and me, and our Creator, and all that was created.

chapter 13

the Final Call

13.1   The final call of this Treatise is, in contrast to those put forth previously, a personal call from me to you. By now you have seen that your fears of losing your Self to God were unfounded. By now you have seen that your Self does not need to stand separate and alone in order to be fulfilled under the mantle of individuality. You have been told to put on a new mantle, a new identity. What does this mean?

13.2   Now that you have been made ready, I am ready to return you to your Self. Now that you have been made ready, it is time for us to have a personal relationship. We have, within these lessons, taken you far from your personal self, and I, as your teacher, have all but discounted the personal self I experience in relationship with you. Now, in unity, we are ready to be personal again.

13.3   While the personal self is the subject of the next treatise, this is my invitation to you, specifically, to enter into a holy and personal relationship with me, specifically. While you are here, you have a persona. While this persona is no longer an ego self but a Christ self, it is still a persona. This is the you who laughs and loves and cries and shares with friends in a world now different than the one you once perceived. I know of this world and I am here to guide you through it. I, too, am friend to you.

13.4   I am the corrector of false thinking because I lived among you as a thinking being. Think not that I was different than you and you will realize that we are truly one in being with our Father. As you move into the world with the end of the time of separation and the beginning of the time of unity taking place around you, practice the beliefs that have been put forth in this treatise. Know that, in the time of unity, the truth will be shared by all.

13.5   Call upon your relationship with me to aid you, as I call upon you to assist me in calling all of our brothers and sisters to their return to unity. We call to one another in gratitude. This is the attitude of the wholehearted, the place from which all calls are sounded and received, the place where the true thinking of those united in mind and heart arises. Gratitude is the recognition of the state of grace in which you exist here and remain forever beyond all time and the passing of all form. It is an attitude of praise and thankfulness that flows between us now. The light of heaven shines not down upon you but is given and received in equal exchange by all who in creation exist together in oneness eternal.

13.6   Forget not who you truly are, but forget not also to be in joy in your experience here. Remember that the seriousness with which you once looked at life is of the ego. Drape your persona in a mantle of peace and joy. Let who you are shine through the personal self who continues to walk this world a while longer. Listen for my voice as I guide you to your purpose here and linger with you in this time to end all time. We are here, together, in love, to share love. This is not such a frightening task. Let fear go and walk with me now. Our journey together is just beginning as we return to the premise put forth in *A Treatise on the Art of Thought*, that of the elevation of form.

$\mathcal{A}$ Treatise on the
PERSONAL SELF

The Third Treatise

chapter 1

True and False Representation

1.1   The personal self exists as the self you present to others. This is the only way in which the personal self will continue to exist following the completion and the integration of this course. Previously, the personal self that you presented to others represented an ego self who you believed yourself to be. Now the ego has been separated from the personal self so that you may claim your personal self again and present to others a true representation of who you are.

1.2   While still a representation, there is a huge difference between true representation and false representation.

1.3   The false representation of the ego as the self is what has led to the world you see. A true representation of the Self that you are is what we work toward in this treatise and will lead to true vision and to a new world.

1.4   A representation of the truth not only reveals the truth but becomes the truth. A representation of what is not the truth reveals only illusion and becomes illusion. Thus, as your personal self becomes a representation of the truth it will become who you are in truth.

1.5   As with much of our previous work, the first step in advancing toward this goal is in developing an awareness of what is not the truth. While the ability to distinguish between the true and the untrue has been repeatedly discussed as the ability to separate fear from love, further guidelines are needed.

1.6   You who have spent most of your life representing the ego have but given a face to illusion and made it seem real. When I say that you have represented the ego, what I mean is that the personal self, as represented by your body, while adhering to the ego's thought system, became an ego-self or an unreal self. An unreal self cannot help but exist in an unreal reality. It is as if you have been an actor upon a stage, the part you play as unreal as the setting on which you play it. Yet there is a "you" who has been playing the part, a part that, while developed under the ego's direction, still allowed for bits and pieces of who you are to be seen, felt, and acknowledged.

1.7   The ego's thought system has been replaced by the thought system of unity and you are left, perhaps, feeling unsure of the part you are now to play. There is not one of you who has not begun to experience the transformation that is, in truth, occurring, although you may not as yet have seen the changes you are experiencing as the transformation to which you have been called. These changes, perhaps, seem like little things, a shift in attitude here, a change in behavior there. But I assure you that these changes are mighty and are but the result of the change in cause that has occurred through your learning of this Course.

1.8   I began this treatise by saying that the personal self exists as the self you present to others and that this is the only way in which the personal self will continue to exist. This statement implies and acknowledges your previous belief in a personal self who existed as more than a representation. While when joined with truth, this representation will be acknowledged as what it is *and* as the truth of who you are, to erroneously have seen your former representation of illusion as the truth of who you are is what has led to your perception of the world of suffering and strife that you have seen.

1.9   This change that is in the process of coming about has to do with awareness. When you become aware of the personal self as a representation, you become aware of the Self whom the personal self is representing. To have believed that the personal self, as a representation of the ego, was who you were, was an illusion that blocked awareness of your true Self from your mind. Your true Self is now ready to come out of the mist of illusion in which it was hidden and to be represented in truth by the form you occupy and have previously seen as the reality of your self.

1.10   To say that the personal self will now exist only as the self you present to others is to say that the personal self will now cease to be seen as your reality or identity.

1.11   To say that the personal self is the only self that existed and that you presented to others in the past is quite a different statement and has a totally different meaning. The personal self you once presented to others as "who you were" was a self who existed in time, who believed that the self of the past made up the self of the present, and that the self of the present made up the self of the future. The personal self you presented to others in the past was a chosen self and never a whole self as evidenced by the variety of selves you saw yourself to be. The personal self of the past was a self of roles, each one as learned as that which an actor might portray. You saw nothing more amiss in being a professional self in one instance and a social self in another, a parent in one role and a friend in another, than you did in defining a past self, a present self, and a future self. The greatest distinction of all was between the private self and the public self, as if who you were to yourself and who you presented yourself to be, could be two completely different selves. Even within the illusion in which you existed there was a self kept hidden.

1.12   To become a whole self, with no parts hidden, a self with no *parts* in truth, is the task that I set before you and am here to help you fulfill. I can do this because I accomplished this, both in life and in all time and time beyond time, making you, along with me, the accomplished. The accomplished Self is the Christ. Your remembrance of the Christ-Self has abolished the ego-self and allows us to begin the lessons of the personal self.

1.13 We could not begin the curriculum here because you would have been unable, without the lessons of this Course, to distinguish the personal self from the ego-self. There is a danger even now in focusing upon the self of the body, as this self has been so long bound to the ego-self. Even with the ego once and finally vanquished, the patterns of the ego's thought system remain to be undone. This is atonement. We work now to correct the errors of the past in the present, the only place where such work can be done. We work with what we have, a form fully able to represent the truth and, in so doing, we bring the truth to life and life to the truth.

chapter 2

the Purpose of Representation

2.1   What purpose would it serve to have anything exist only as a representation? We might think of this in terms of original purpose and the original purpose of representation being to share the Self in a new way. Expressions you call art are desires to share the Self in a new way. These expressions you call art are expressions of a self who observes and interacts in relationship. They are not expressions that remain contained within who you are or who you think yourself to be. They are not expressions of the self-alone. They are not expressions of the self-alone in terms you might consider autobiographical, and they are not expressions of the self-alone that you would consider the self in separation. They are rather expressions of the Self-in-union — expressions of what the Self sees, feels, envisions, imagines in relationship.

2.2   What purpose has art? While art is but a representation of what the artist chooses to share, few of us would call these representations useless or without value. Art is a representation, but it also becomes something in truth, something that has been named "art." Art becomes something in truth by expanding awareness, or in other words, by making something known. This is what true relationship does and is it's purpose as well as what it is.

2.3   While we have said you chose the separation, it has not been said that this choice was the choice it has been made to seem. You chose to represent yourself in a new way, to express yourself in a new way, to share yourself in a new way. The choice to represent your Self in form was a choice for separation but not because separation itself was desired as you have assumed. This is the assumption you have accepted in much the same way you have accepted your free will as that which allows you to be separate from and independent of God. Once this assumption was accepted, the duality of your existence became paramount. It became the only means you saw of deciphering the world around you and your role within it. Separation, aloneness, independence, individuality, became the purpose you assumed rather than the purpose you started out to achieve — that of a new way of expression in a form that would expand awareness, through relationship, of self and others. You chose a means of creation...as God chose a means of creation. That means of creation is separation, becoming separate (the observer as well as the observed) so as to extend creation through relationship (of the observer and the observed).

2.4   While much time was spent discussing within this Course the choice you but think you made, this discussion was necessary only in the same terms that made it necessary to thoroughly discuss the ego's thought system. What you believe about yourself is part of the foundation that has been built around this system. Now, along with the beliefs put forth in the Treatise on Unity, you are asked to accept a new belief regarding the choice we have called the separation, a choice you have deemed as sin.

2.5   While you have believed you are the self of the ego, you have believed in a need to both glorify the self and denigrate the self. These beliefs have shaped your dualistic view of the world and all that exists with you within it. For every "glory," gift, or success you have achieved, you have believed in a corresponding cost that was, in essence, a cost that came at the expense or denigration of the self. You believed that for every gain there was also a loss. For you believed that every step in the advancement of your separated state was a step away from God and your real Self. This belief was based in logic — but in

110

the logic of the illusion — a logic that had you believing that you chose to separate from God out of defiance and a desire to be one with God no longer. This could not be further from the truth, and is the cause of all your suffering, for contained within this belief was the belief that with each successful step toward independence came a corresponding step away from God. As independence seemed to be your purpose here, you could not keep yourself from attempts to advance in this direction. Neither could you keep from punishing yourself for this advancement.

2.6   We leave all of this behind now as we advance toward truth through returning to original purpose. Your return to your original purpose eliminates the concept of original sin and leaves you blameless. It is from this blameless or unaltered state that your personal self can begin to represent the truth, for it leaves untruth, or the ego, behind. It is only this one, unaltered Self that *is* the truth of who you are and who your brothers and sisters are. This is what is meant by oneness. This is what is meant by unity.

2.7   The truth has as many ways of being represented as does illusion.

2.8   Just as artistic representations of illusion are sometimes called art, representations of the self of illusion have been called the Self without this being so. In each, however, is the self you believe is real revealed. Thus, not all that is called "art" is art, and not all that you call "self" is Self, even while both may represent the truth as you perceive it. Representing the truth as you perceive it to be has been the righteous work of many who have caused great harm to others and the world. There is no truth to be found in illusion and so no representations of perceived truth, no matter how intensely they have been championed, have truly altered effect for they have not altered cause.

111

2.9   There is no right or wrong in art, and there is no right or wrong, no good or bad in regard to the self, but there are accurate and inaccurate representations of the truth. Inaccurate representations of the truth simply have no meaning. No matter how much one might try to find meaning in the meaningless it will not be found. The meaningless has no ability to change the meaning of truth. And so your Self has remained unaltered as has all to which you have assigned inaccurate meaning.

2.10   Thus you stand at the beginning, with a Self now devoid of the meaninglessness you but attempted to assign to it. You stand empty of untruth and about to embark on the journey of truth. You stand in the transformational moment between the unreal and the real. All you await is an idea, a remembrance of the original idea about your personal self.

2.11   This memory lies within your heart and has the ability to turn the image you have made into a reflection of the love that abides with it in holiness that is beyond your current ability to imagine. It is impossible for you to imagine this holiness with the concepts of the thought system you heretofore have relied upon. This thought system has allowed only the acceptance of a reality within certain parameters for it has not allowed you to imagine being able to take steps "back" to the God you believe you left in defiance or the Self you believe you abandoned there. Be truthful with yourself now and realize that what I speak of here is known to you. Realize that you *know* that it is not God who abandoned you, but you who abandoned your Self and God. Give up your desire to think that if you did such a thing there was a reason for you to have done so. How many times have you asked yourself why you would have chosen separation if there had not been a *reason* for you to do so? Realize that a reason has been given here and that this reason, while perfectly believable, is not one that includes a need to abandon your Self or God. Why should you be more inclined to believe that you left paradise to live a while in a form that would cause you much suffering and strife, for the sole reason of being separate from that which you long to return to? The only alternative has seemed to be a belief in a God who would banish you from paradise for your sins. We have worked, thus far, to change your idea of a vengeful God. Now we work to change your idea of a vengeful self. For what else would such a self be?

2.12   This is so important for you to grasp that I return you to our comparison of the family of man to the family of God, as well as to our discussion of the return of the prodigal sons and daughters of God. This discussion may have seemed to accept the idea of a self as highly developed as an adolescent child, a self who would willingly choose to explore independence, no matter what the cost. But what this discussion examined was the reality you chose to believe in: the reality of an ego-self, and a self-concept seemingly stuck in an adolescent phase of development. The ego-self's only desire was for you to "grow up" into its version of an independent being...no matter what the cost.

2.13   While you may be happily congratulating yourself on leaving such adolescent thinking behind, this thinking must be quickly replaced with a new idea about yourself or its hold on you will remain.

chapter 3

the True Self

3.1　Your personal self is dear to you and dear to me as well. I have always loved you because I have always recognized you. What cannot be recognized or known cannot be loved. While your ego has not been loveable, you have always been. Here is where you need realize that the personal self that is dear to you is not your ego-self and never has been.

3.2　All of your personal characteristics are nothing more than a persona that has served the ego faithfully. All of your traits have been chosen either in accordance with the ego's desires or in opposition to them. Whether they be in accord or in opposition, their source has still been the ego. These traits, whether you see them as good or bad or somewhere in between, are what you have seen as making you loveable or unlovable. Yet you have also often made them challenges to love, saying in effect to those who love you, love me in spite of these traits that are not loveable and then I will know your love is true. You make this same statement to yourself as well, seemingly called to continuously challenge your own lovability.

3.3　As much as you fear disappointment for yourself and let this fear keep you from much you would desire, you fear as much or more your ability to disappoint others or to "let them down." Some of you carefully constructed your lives to leave as little room as possible for disappointment to affect it or others you hold dear. Some of you have seemed to do the opposite, despite your best intentions calling disappointment to yourself and being constantly under the pall of having disappointed others. Still others have always found their lives to be beyond their efforts at control and long ago gave up trying. Most of you fall somewhere in between, living a life full of good intentions and effort and being surprised neither by what seems to work nor what seems to fail.

3.4   It is your self, who, more often than not, you blamed for all of your misfortune. You would have liked to be strong and capable and hated your own weakness. You would have liked to be even-tempered and hated the moods that seemed to come over you without cause. You did not understand when illness or depression stood in the way of your desires or the plans of others and let such circumstances fill you with self-loathing.

3.5   You created a society that reflected this hatred of the self and that functioned on finding blame for every misfortune. Your illnesses became the result of behaviors ranging from smoking, to too little exercise. Your accidents caused lawsuits where blame could be rightly placed. Your depression was blamed on the past. Even your successes were often claimed to be at the expense of another or to have come in spite of failings most severe. While society would seem to have done so much to cause your unhappiness, and while you have in turn blamed it as much as it blamed you, you never blamed anything quite as much as you blamed yourself.

3.6   This is the vengeful self that we eliminate now. You have, in truth, replaced judgment with forgiveness, but you have not yet fully forgiven yourself. This statement may sound incongruous, for how could you have replaced judgment with forgiveness and not forgiven yourself? What this means is that you have replaced judgment with forgiveness as a belief. You have put this belief into practice in each instance where you have seen it to be needed. Yet you continue to fail to recognize your need to replace judgment with forgiveness when it comes to yourself. You have not realized how much you still consider unlovable about yourself. This does not mean that you are not loveable, only that you have not fully recognized your true Self. Until you fully recognize your Self, you cannot fully love yourself. Until you fully love, you do not love in truth.

3.7   Both God and love are found in relationship where the truth becomes known to you. When the truth becomes known to you, you know God, for you know love.   Beliefs, and especially the changed beliefs we have worked together to integrate into your thought system, are only a first step, a step toward holy relationship.   These new beliefs of your new thought system must be wholehearted.   In other words, they cannot be beliefs that exist only in your mind, a new philosophy to be applied to life. They must exist in your heart. And how can they exist in the heart of an unlovable self?

3.8   You cannot think your way to the new life that calls to you. You can only get there by being who you are in truth.

3.9   I have always loved you for I have always recognized you. While your recognition of your Self has come a long way through your learning of this Course, your self is still seen as a stumbling block. You might think that were you able to live in some ideal community, away from all that has brought you to where you now are, you might be able to put the beliefs of this Course into practice. If not quite this drastic, your thoughts might tell you that if you were in another job, devoid of certain familial responsibilities, or of the need to provide for financial obligations, you would be much better suited to putting these beliefs into practice. Or you might look at your behaviors, your habits, your general personality, and simply declare yourself unsuitable for further learning.   Whether you think such thoughts consciously or not, there is a part of you that still believes you are not good enough to be the "good" self you believe this Course calls you to be. Most of you have now believed you are "good enough" for days or hours or moments, but something always and eventually calls you back to the idea that you are not good enough or that you do not want to put the effort into being good enough. Like a person who believes she has a weight problem and knows a diet would be "good" for her, the diet is often rejected because failure is deemed a certainty. While you continue to see the call of this Course as a call to goodness, you will surely fail.

3.10   The Self that I recognize as You is not other than who you are but who you are. All that has ever been other than who you are is the ego. The ego is gone. The ego was simply your idea of who you were. This idea was a complex set of judgments, of good and bad, right and wrong, worthy and unworthy, a list as endless as it was worthless. Realize now the worthlessness of this idea and let it go.

chapter 4

the Dismantling of Illusion

4.1   This is not a self-help course but just the opposite. This Course has stated time and time again that you cannot learn on your own and that resigning as your own teacher is the only way to learn a new curriculum. This Course will not call you to effort of any kind. It will not tell you to leave behind your addictions or to go on a diet or a fast. It will not even tell you to be kind. It does not tell you to be responsible and does not chide your irresponsibility. It does not claim that you were once bad but that by following these tenets you can become good. It gives no credence and no blame to any past cause for your depression, anxiety, meanness, illness or insanity. It merely calls you to sanity by calling you to let go of illusion in favor of the truth.

4.2   The sameness that this Course calls you to is not a sameness of body or of habit. It asks not for monks or clones. It asks not that you give up anything but illusion, which is the giving up of nothing.

4.3   Before we can go on you must take all such ideas from your mind. Such ideas are not small matters. Ideas are the foundation of the self. You cannot have an idea of goodness without having an idea of evil. You cannot have an idea of an ideal state without having an idea of a state that is not ideal. You cannot have an idea you call "right" without believing in an idea that can be "wrong."

4.4   The ego made such ideas necessary for the idea of the ego was "wrong" or inaccurate. The only way to bring that inaccuracy to light was through contrast.

118

4.5   To function from an inaccurate foundation was to build upon that foundation. Building a structure with a foundation that would not support it was the folly that the ego made of life. The only way for such an error to be seen as an error is through its dysfunction.

4.6   The only way to correct such an error is to dismantle the structure and begin again with a foundation capable of being built upon. This is what we have done. We have taken away the foundation of illusion, the one error that became the basis of all that came after it. You cannot make another error such as this for it is the one error. Does it not make sense that the only error possible is that of not being who you are?

4.7   You can dismantle the ego and build another in its place and this has at times been done in the individual with great training, as in military training, or in cases of great abuse when a second ego personality is developed to "save" the first. The ego has also been dismantled and rebuilt over time and been seen as the rise and fall of civilizations. The only replacement that will work is the replacement of illusion with the truth. The very purpose of this treatise is to prevent the replacement of illusion with illusion, or one ego-self with another. The training of this Course, while gentle in nature, has been great, as great as that of any military training, as great as any emotional trauma that has left one in a state of emptiness. This is, in effect, the state in which you currently find yourself.

4.8   I repeat, and will do so again and again, that the ego-self is gone from you. Whether you fully realize this or not matters not. This the Course has accomplished. Now the choice is before you to do one of two things: to proceed with love or with fear. If you proceed with fear you will assemble a new ego-self, an ego-self that perhaps will seem superior to the old, but which will nonetheless still be an ego-self. If you proceed with love, you will come to know your Christ-Self.

chapter 5

Original Purpose

5.1   You have just been told that you now exist in a state of emptiness. This is not a state to be feared. Yet it is this fear of emptiness that has, in the past, made those who have experienced it rush to find the easiest and most available replacement (the ego or that which has become familiar if not known). While few of you have ever before reached the emptiness caused by the complete absence of the ego, just as few of you have never felt some sort of absence. All the lessons you have drawn to yourself in your lifetime have worked toward this absence in the hopes of filling the emptiness with the fullness of the truth.

5.2   As with the gentle learning of this Course, not all emptiness has come to you at the hands of suffering. Each time you have "fallen" in love you have emptied a space for love to fill. Each time you have felt true devotion you have emptied a space for love to fill. You have been emptied of the ego-self as creative moments of inspiration filled you and emptied of the ego-self in moments of connection with God.

5.3   Conversely, you have been emptied by the lessons of grief as the loss of love has led to a loss of self. You have been emptied by a loss of self due to illness or addiction, depression or even physical exhaustion. All these things you have brought to yourself for they have been the only way past the ego's guarded gate.

5.4   You have tried to live in a house built on a faulty foundation, attempting to make-do with what you have.   All your time was spent in making repairs and this time spent kept you too busy to see the light that was always visible through the cracked and peeling walls that you built.   That you would eventually call to yourself a fire that would burn these walls to ash or a flood that would wash them away, was as much a part of the survival mechanism of your real Self as was the rush to rebuild a part of the survival mechanism of the ego-self.

5.5   All this you have already tried to do; these lessons you have already tried to learn. This Course has come so that these many things that you have tried need not be repeated, just as the crucifixion came to end the need to learn through suffering and death.

5.6   The story that I lived was appropriate for the time in which I lived it and has an appropriateness that continues even now. I walked the earth in order to reveal a God of love. The question of the time, a question still much in evidence, was how mighty could God's love be if it were given to a people who suffered. The answer was that God's love was so mighty that he would even allow the death of his only son to redeem the world.

5.7   The death of an only son, then as now, would be seen as a sacrifice of enormous proportions, the greatest sacrifice of all. But the story was not one of sacrifice, but one of gift giving. The greatest gift of all was given, the gift of redemption. The gift of redemption was the gift of an end to pain and suffering and a beginning of resurrection and new life. It was a gift meant to empty the world of the ego-self and to allow the personal self to live on as the one true Self, the one true Son of God. The gift of redemption was given once and for all. It is the gift of restoration to original purpose. Without there having been an original purpose worthy of God's son, the crucifixion would have ended life in form and returned the sons of man to the formless. Instead, the sons of man were freed to pursue their original purpose.

5.8   This story has been repeated endlessly in time, in time extending both forward and back. Each father's son will die. Yet this means not what you have taken it to mean — an endless series of generations passing. What this means is that in each the ego will die and the Self be reborn to life eternal. Without rebirth of the Self, the original purpose goes unfulfilled. Since God is original purpose, original cause, the origin of Self and of relationship, original purpose cannot go unfulfilled. What this means is that the illusion will be no more and truth will reign. Such is the reign of God.

chapter 6

the Desire for Reward

6.1   Can you give up your desire for reward? To give up
your desire for reward is to give up a childish desire that has
become like unto a plague among you. While many of you see
it not, everything you do is based upon desire for reward. This
is your desire to be given to in return for what you give. It
stems from your idea of yourself as a "child" of God, and a
notion that would seem to suggest that the child is less than the
parent. Although you see yourself as the child of your mother
and father, this notion of your self as child has not made you
cling to a childish image of yourself as less than what your
parents are.   While you may still desire recognition and
affirmation from them, this is not the same as the "rewards"
you seek, some of you from God, some from life, some from
fate. No matter who it is you think is in charge of rewarding
you, the attitude that causes you to desire reward is what must
be done without.

6.2   This may seem a step back from the lofty heights we
have just traveled, discussing the reign of God and the meaning
of life and death. But this is one of the key ideas that will keep
you from yourself, and has much to do with your former
notions of God and your own self. It is an idea that has been
transferred to all of life, much as the idea of an unlovable self
was transferred into all areas of life without your realization.

6.3   Reward is intricately tied to your notions of being good,
performing deeds of merit, and taking care of, or surviving the
many details that seem to make it possible for you to live within
your world. The idea of reward also transfers to ideas related

to comparison, as lack of reward in one instance and reward given in another, is the cause of much of the bitterness that exists within your hearts.

6.4   While many of you who have read this far and learned this much may not be those whose bitterness is mighty and held tightly to themselves, bitterness must still be discussed, for while bitterness remains, vengeance will remain. You have been shown that God is not a God of vengeance but you are still in the process of learning that your Self is not vengeful. The ego has given you many reasons to be distrustful of your Self, beginning with the idea of your abandonment here. Since the ego is a chosen self and a learned self, there has always been just enough room within the ego's thought system to keep within you the idea of a self the ego is not. Thus has the ego had a self to blame for everything, including your very existence. This blame is as old as time itself, and the cause of bitterness being able to exist, even within your hearts.

6.5   While the untrue cannot exist with the true, what I am calling here *bitterness* is all that you have forced, through sheer strength of will, to pierce the holiness of your hearts. Bitterness and the idea of vengeance go hand-in-hand. This is the idea of "an eye for an eye" or the exact opposite of the idea of "turning the other cheek." While this may seem like the very idea of evil which I have denied the existence of, it is not evil but bitterness. You may believe that bitterness is just another word, another label for the evil you have always been convinced existed in the hearts of some, but even being that it is "just" another word, it is one chosen to introduce an idea of such fallacy that it rivals only the ego in its destructive potential. Bitterness is to your heart what the ego has been to your mind. It is the one false idea that has entered this holiest of places, this abode of Christ, this bridge between the human and the divine. It exists not in some but in all, as the ego has existed not in some but in all. Like the ego, it has not caused you to be unlovable or unrecognizable. But it has become, like the ego, so much a part of your reality, that it must, like the ego, be consciously left behind.

6.6   Bitterness, as the word implies, is something taken into the self much as the bitter herbs of scripture illustrated. Many rights and rituals exist for the purification of the unclean but I assure you that you are not unclean and that none can cleanse bitterness from the heart without your choice. The time of tenderness began your release of bitterness and but made you ready for this choice. Choose now to leave your desire for reward, all of your reasons for bitterness, and bitterness itself behind. Bring bitterness no longer to the dwelling place of Christ and we will seal the place of its entrance with the sweetness of love so that bitterness will be no more.

chapter 7

the Explosion of Belief

7.1   As you have seen by now, we have moved from talking of beliefs in the Treatise on Unity, to speaking here of ideas. God's thought of you is an idea of absolute truth. Your existence derives from this idea and this truth. The ego's existence derived from your idea of a separated self, a thought, or idea, of absolute untruth. The ego's thought system then formed beliefs that supported the initial idea of the separation. Where is there a corresponding belief system that formed around the idea of God?

7.2   A belief system is not needed for the truth. Thus you can see that the beliefs put forth in the Treatise on Unity are necessary only to return you to the truth. Since there are no beliefs that represent the truth of who you are and who God is, we speak now of ideas or thoughts. If you believe that God created you with a thought or idea, then you can begin to see the power of thought. If you can believe that you created the ego with a thought or an idea, you can see where the power of thought is your power as well as God's.

7.3   While there is no need for a belief system and no belief system that *can* represent the truth, you have been told that *you* can represent the truth here. You cannot do this with beliefs but you can do this with ideas. Ideas leave not their source and thus your inaccurate ideas about yourself have their cause within you, as does your ability to change this cause and its effects.

7.4   You are who you are and remain endlessly who you are, even here within the human experience. This is the idea that is beyond compare as you are beyond compare and the truth is beyond compare. This is the only idea that holds true meaning and so all meaning is found within it. Thus we start with this idea.

7.5   The only thing within the human experience that made you incapable of representing who you are in truth was the ego. The only thing within the human experience that deprived the human experience of meaning was the ego. With the ego gone, you are perfectly capable of representing the truth of who you are, and of returning to an existence that is meaningful.

7.6   You have formerly been capable of representing who you are only within illusion, for this was the abode in which you resided. Illusion has been to you like a house with many doors. You have chosen many doors to the same house and but thought them to offer different things, only to find that the house you entered was still the same house, the house of illusion. You took yourself into these many rooms and in some you were even capable of representing your true Self. This representation of the true Self within the house of illusion was like an explosion happening there. For a moment, the floorboards shook, the walls quaked, the lights dimmed. All those within the house became aware of something happening there. All attention turned toward the explosion but its source could not be found.

7.7   In the aftermath of the explosion, the representation of the true Self settled like dust, and all the attention fell upon it. A great scrambling ensued as the recognition dawned on those who looked, that treasures were to be found there. One found art and another religion, one found poetry and another music, one seized upon a single thought and through its extrapolation founded one science or another. In all of the excitement the matter of the source of the explosion was dismissed.

7.8   Thus has been the best of what you call life within the illusion.

7.9   Now you have seized upon even this idea and called it not treasure but theory and related it to the origins of the universe itself, and still you see not the source.   There is a reason for this. The reason is that the Source cannot be found within the house of illusion. The Source can only be found from within the house of truth.

7.10   The house of truth is within you and we have just unlocked its doors.

chapter 8

the House of Truth

8.1   The Kingdom of God is the House of Truth. Or better said, the House of Truth has been called the Kingdom of God. I remind you, once again, that what you have called things are but representations too and that we move now beyond representations to meaning so that what you represent will move beyond representations to the truth. Realize here the subtle difference between a symbol that represents the truth, and the truth, for this is what we work toward. Symbols are needed only in the house of illusion, just as are beliefs. The most enlightened among you have beautifully symbolized or represented the truth within the house of illusion. These symbols or representations have been of great service and have caused the very explosions that have rocked your faulty foundation. To work toward being a representation of such great power is still a worthy goal and many of you have reached this power. You can see why this power has been necessary and continues to be necessary. But to stop at this dismantling power is not enough. To stop at this dismantling power would be to leave the world in its present condition and your brothers and sisters scrambling in the dust. The work that is upon you now is that of replacing the house of illusion once and for all with the house of truth. The work that is upon you now is that of revelation of the Source.

8.2   If the Source of Truth is within you, then it is your own revelation toward which we work. Never forget that establishing your identity has been the only aim of this entire course of study. Realize how often you have forgotten this despite the many repetitions of our aim and you will be more aware of your resistance and your need to let it go.

8.3   This resistance is the reason you have been taken on such a long journey before we ever once talked of an idea as crucial as that of bitterness. Bitterness has been a source of resistance as strong as that of the ego and more deeply felt. Bitterness is to your heart what the ego has been to your mind. Bitterness has to do with your feelings more so than your thoughts. The ego but played upon these feelings, using them as building blocks for its thought system. As long as you carry this bitterness within you, you will remain in the house of illusion for your feelings are as real to you as have been the thoughts of your ego-mind. While anything other than the truth remains real to you, your house of illusion will remain a real structure, a structure that keeps you from the truth as surely as would iron bars keep you within its rooms.

8.4   Although at this moment it may be hard for you to conceive of the idea of bitterness as something that you are attached to, I want you to think of attachments for a time and see how bitterness does indeed fit into this category. Bitterness is an idea intrinsically tied to the personal self and the experience of the personal self. Whether you believe the personal self is comprised of the one identity you now hold or the identity of many past lives, the identity you hold in this time and this place still believes in its own history and that of those who came before it. These beliefs hold the seeds of bitterness, the angst you feel toward God, and toward brothers and sisters both alive and dead.

8.5   These are the beliefs that would say that you, and all of those who came before you, have been falsely made to suffer, a suffering for which you see no rationale. Those who believe in past lives have also often adopted beliefs regarding choice and believe that choices for suffering were made for some greater good or to repay debts of the past. The only choice that has been made is that of attachment to the human form. The choice that hasn't been made is the choice to leave it behind. The choice that has been made is to believe in a savior who could have, but did not, keep you from this suffering. The choice that has not been made is the choice to believe in the Christ-self who is the only savior, rather than the ego-self, which is all you have needed saving from.

8.6   What happens when you believe that the choice to suffer, as well as the choice to leave suffering behind, has always been found within? Who then are you to be angry with for all that has occurred? Do you blame yourself and your ancestors for the history, both ancient and recent, that you think you would have given anything to change? Do you look upon the ill and blame them for their illness? Do you not look upon all suffering and feel bitter at your own inability to relieve it? And do you not attempt to see it not and then blame yourself for looking the other way?

8.7   As was said in *A Course of Love*, the idea of suffering is what has gone so wrong within God's creation. As was said in *A Treatise on the Art of Thought,* the idea of love can replace the idea of suffering, but it is chosen not because of the suffering that seems to make no sense of love. Bitterness is the cause of this inability to make a new choice and what keeps the cycle of suffering in motion.

8.8   Remaining attached to bitterness is a reflection of the disbelief that one person, and surely not you, can make a difference. If you could relieve the world of suffering you would, but to try and fail is too heartbreaking. Why should you not be bitter when you and all of those you love will surely suffer and eventually die? Why should you not be bitter when you believe you are powerless? How difficult it is to believe that you need not change the world but only your own self. How difficult to imagine that this one change could bring about all the changes you would imagine even an army of angels could not bring about. While such a thought remains inconceivable to you it will not come to be.

8.9   As the representations of the true self within the house of illusion caused explosions and a fall-out of treasure, the representation of the true Self within the house of truth will cause the creation of the new.

8.10   Your ancestors could not have imagined all that the explosions in the house of illusion have wrought. Treasures that you now enjoy would have seemed like miracles to them.

8.11   Within the fallout of treasure, what was looked for was found. If what was looked for were means of making life easier, why not the idea of machinery and tools that would seem to make it so? If what was looked for was a means of finding simple pleasures in a harsh world, why not ideas of entertainment that would seem to provide them. People suffering from disease: why not cures for those diseases?

8.12   People have looked for what they have imagined it was possible to find. Why would you look for an end to suffering if you felt this was impossible? Much better to look for cures and treatments than for an end to what but seemed endless. Could suffering really have gone on for countless ages simply due to your inability to birth the idea of an end to suffering?

8.13   Has not a part of you always known that suffering does not have to be, even while you have accepted that it is? Let us now put an end to this acceptance through the birth of a new idea.

chapter 9

To Dwell in the House of Truth

9.1   This idea is an idea of love. It is an idea that makes perfect sense and it is its very sense that makes it seem meaningless in a world gone mad. It is an idea that says *only that which comes from love is real*. It is an idea that says *only that which fits within the laws of love is reality*. It is an idea that says *all that love would not create does not exist*. It is an idea that says that *if you live from love and within love's laws you will create only love*. It is an idea that accepts that this can be done and can be done by you in the here and now. To accept these ideas without accepting their ability to be applied is to change your beliefs without changing your ideas. This many have done. This you surely do not want to do.

9.2   While you cannot see, right now, the chain of events that will make these ideas of love into a new reality, you can trust that it will be there spreading out like a web, much as did the ego's ideas of separation. These ideas are not learned ideas, and so they will not take time to spread through learning, as did the ego's ideas.

9.3   Ideas of love, or the truth, are joined in unity and exist in relationship. All of the ideas within the house of illusion were contained within it and held together by the learned ideas of the ego thought-system. Now you must imagine yourself walking outside of the doors of this house of illusion and finding a completely new reality beyond its walls. You might think, at first, that you are in a place so foreign that you must immediately begin to learn again, starting with the smallest building blocks of knowledge, as if learning a new alphabet. Yet you soon will find that this new reality is known to you and requires no new learning at all. You will be tempted, at first, to see things that are like onto those within the house of illusion and call them what you called them once before. But here you will find yourself gently corrected and, when this correction is given, you will not doubt it but will remember that it is the truth you but had forgotten.

9.4   You will see that the house of illusion was just a structure built within the universe of truth and that the universe of truth contains everything within its benevolent embrace. No one stands beyond the embrace of love and you will be glad to see that those who remain within the house of illusion cannot escape love's presence.

9.5   You will be tempted, nonetheless, to re-enter the house of illusion, if only to grasp the hands of those you love and gently tug them through its doors. You will be able to take note of the explosions happening within and will want to return to add your own to those going on inside, thinking that with the force of one more, maybe the walls will finally come tumbling down and those inside be held within illusion no more. This was the work of many who came before you but the time of such work for you has passed. Many remain to shake the walls of illusion. Few stand beyond it to beckon to those within.

9.6   The paradise that is the truth seems to lie far beyond the house of illusion in the valley of death. Survivors of near death experiences have eased the fears of many but made many more long for life after death rather than life. You who have followed me beyond the walls of the house of illusion are now called to begin the act of revealing and creating anew the life of heaven on earth.

9.7   This is the pilgrimage I set you on, as real as those who in the time of Moses journeyed through the desert to the promised land. That journey remained metaphorical because it did not pass beyond the arena of beliefs into the arena of ideas. The Israelites believed in a promised land but they did not dwell in it. You are called to dwell in the promised land, the House of Truth.

chapter 10

An Exercise in Forgetting

10.1   *A Course of Love* talked much of remembering. Now we must talk about forgetting. While nothing need be given up to enter the house of truth, or to encounter the truth, you must realize that while meaninglessness exists within your mind, you will be working still to replace it with meaning rather than allowing the meaning that exists in everything to be remembered or known. Thus are more practical lessons needed in regard to the life of the body that you now will let serve our cause of creating heaven on earth.

10.2   The first lesson is offered as an exercise in forgetting. As often as is possible within your daily life, I ask you to forget as much of what you have learned as you are able.

10.3   The first thing I ask you to forget is your need to find a place where blame can be placed. You who have been waiting to get to the "hard part" of this course of study may find it here. The idea of blame is incongruous with the idea of a benevolent creator and a benevolent creation and as such is the only blasphemy. To blame yourself is as senseless as blaming others and your inclination to place blame upon yourself must be given up. When it is said that you are the cause, it is not meant that you are to blame for anything. Although many a child has been blamed for his or her failure to learn, blaming yourself is as uncalled for as is blaming a child for lessons yet to be learned.

10.4   Taking away the idea of placing blame will change your thought processes beyond your wildest imagining. You will be surprised at how many times you will recognize blame where before you saw it not, just as in the beginning, you came to recognize fears that you previously hadn't seen as fears. And, just as when you recognize what it is you fear you can bring those concerns to love, you can now do so with blame. All you need do is catch yourself in the act of placing blame and say to yourself, "I was placing blame again and I choose to do so no longer." You need not spend any more time with blame than this and I offer you no word or sentiment to replace it. I ask you simply to take the thought of it from your mind as quickly as it enters.

10.5   You would find this easier if a replacement were offered, for ridding your mind of blame will leave an empty space you will long to fill. This act of consciously choosing not to place blame will short-circuit the many thoughts that you would attach to this idea, thoughts that have formed a chain-reaction of situations and events, feelings and behaviors that you had no realization were birthed from the idea of blame. Although I offer it not as a replacement, what you will find will come in the place of blame is an idea of acceptance of what is, an idea that is needed now.

10.6   Acceptance of what *is*, is acceptance that whatever is happening in the present moment is a gift and a lesson. What comes as a lesson may not seem like a gift, but all lessons are gifts. While some of these lessons may come in forms that make them seem like lessons of old, they will not be repeats of lessons that have come before. They will not be lessons that you find difficult or distressing if you accept them as lessons and realize that all lessons are gifts. What you have struggled to learn in the past you have struggled with only because you did not realize the nature of the situation as a lesson or recognize that all lessons are gifts.

10.7   This relates to our exercise in forgetting for you must forget the ways in which you have formerly reacted to every situation. Not one situation coming to you now will be a repeat of the past. How can it be, when the past was lived in the house of illusion and the present is lived in the house of truth? Being cognizant of this is the only way that the simultaneous learning and unlearning that was spoken of earlier will be able to be realized. You have passed through your time of unlearning what the past but seemed to teach you. Now, while life may seem much unchanged in its outward appearance, it is up to you to become aware of the total change that has, in truth, taken place.

10.8   Along with forgetting there is another practice that will help you to become aware of this change. While much the same as forgetting, it will seem to have a different process in practice. This is the practice of ceasing to listen to the voice of the ego. While the ego is gone, many of its messages remain within your thoughts like echoes of a former time. These thoughts are remembered messages and so must, like all the rest, be forgotten. The process of forgetting these thought patterns will be only slightly different from forgetting your former reactions to people and situations, and much like forgetting to place blame.

10.9   The first step in being able to forget such thoughts is in recognizing them as separate and distinct from the thoughts of your right mind or Christ-mind. This will be easy because the thoughts of the ego-mind were always harsh with you or with others. The Christ-mind and the thoughts that come from the voice of the Christ-mind will be gentle. The thoughts of the ego-mind will come as disguises to certainty. Given just a little practice, these disguises will be easily seen through and the uncertainty behind them revealed. Thoughts of the Christ-mind will hold a certainty that cannot be disguised. Remember that all doubt is doubt about yourself. You are no longer called to doubt yourself for your Self is now your Christ-Self.

10.10   You will feel for a while as if constant certainty is impossible. This feeling will remain only as long as you remember your past uncertainty. Uncertainty, like the rest of the ego's thought system, was learned. Your true Self has no cause for uncertainty. Thus you are called to forget the uncertainty of the past.

10.11   While these may seem like remedial lessons, they are not. You are no longer called to a time of uncertainty to learn through contrast the lessons of certainty. Realize that this is how you have learned *in the past* and that all that is from the past is what you are being called to forget. When uncertainty arises, you need but remind yourself that the time for uncertainty is past. Uncertainty will not now come to teach you lessons you have already learned but will only visit you as an echo from the past. It is a habit, a pattern of the old thought system. All you must do is not listen to it. Its voice will not be gentle or full of love. Its voice will hold the unmistakable edge of fear.

10.12   Remember that, while gentle, these are and will be *practical* lessons that simply come to show you a new way of living, the way of living in the house of truth. You will not need to learn a foreign *language* to dwell in this new house, but you will need to learn what will at first seem to you a foreign *thought system*. This thought system recognizes no fear nor judgment, no uncertainty nor doubt, no contrast and no division. It is the thought system of unity. It is your true thought system and will be easily remembered once you begin to let it automatically replace the old.

10.13   Think of this for a moment as you would a learned language. If you learned Spanish as a child and then learned and spoke English for many years, you might believe your Spanish to be forgotten. Yet if you were to return to a dwelling where those within it spoke only Spanish, soon your knowledge of Spanish would return to you. For a short while you would have two languages constantly running through your mind and you would be translating one into the other. But eventually, if this situation went on for many years, you might think you had forgotten your ability to understand English.

10.14 What we are doing now is much like translating the learned thought system of the ego into the thought system of the Christ-Self that you but think you have forgotten. As you dwell in the house of truth, if you do not resist unlearning the ego thought system, the thought system of your true Self will quite simply return to your memory. You will soon forget the thought system of the ego-self even though, when encountering those who still use that thought system, you will be able to communicate with them. The ease with which you communicate with them will, however, diminish over time, and you will find yourself continuously teaching the *language* if you will, of the new thought system, for you will have no desire to communicate with anything less.

10.15 You will find that your new *language* will gather people to you in much the way people will gravitate toward beautiful music. Many will be eager to learn what you have remembered because they will realize that the memory of this *language* also exists within them. It will come naturally to you to welcome these back to the common *language* of the mind and heart joined in unity. You will desire more than anything for everyone you encounter to share this remembered language. Some, however, will be resistant.

10.16 This is why we have called these "lessons in forgetting" practical lessons for the life of the body. They are lessons that will soon be translated in another way. These lessons that will enter your mind and heart will, of necessity, need to be translated into the language of the body. While your human form remains, you will be dwelling among those in human form. While the house of illusion still exists, you will continue to encounter those who exist within it. While you continue to encounter those who exist in the house of illusion, you will continue to encounter temptations of the human experience. These are what we will now address.

chapter 11

the Temptations of the Human Experience

11.1   Consciousness is a state of awareness. The statement "I am" is a statement of awareness. It has been seen as a statement of awareness of the self. Those existing within the house of illusion are aware of the self, but are unaware that the self of illusion, the self that exists in illusion, is an illusionary self. This could be further stated as those who exist in the house of illusion are aware of the personal self alone and believe the personal self to be who they are. Further, they believe the personal self to be the truth of the statement, "I am."

11.2   Those existing within the house of truth also feel an awareness of self. Without necessarily being able to put it into words, they no longer feel the statement of "I am" as a statement of the personal self or the self alone. For those existing in the house of truth, "I am" has become something larger, an encompassing recognition of the unity of all things with which the Self co-exists in truth and peace and love.

11.3   These words, *truth* and *peace* and *love*, are interchangeable in the house of truth as their meaning there is the same. These words, like the words *house of truth* represent an awareness of a new reality, a new dwelling place.

11.4   The word *house* as used in the *house of truth* does not represent a structure but a dwelling place. The word *house* as used in the *house of illusion* does represent a structure. The house of illusion is a construction meant to shield the personal self from all that it would fear. The house of truth is the dwelling place of those who no longer live in fear and who have no need for a structure of seeming protection.

11.5   The house of illusion is the stage on which the drama of the human experience has been acted out.

11.6   During the time I spent on earth I did not dwell in the house of illusion but in the house of truth. What this means is that I was aware of the truth and lived by the truth. I was aware of the Peace of God and lived within the Peace of God. I was aware of the Love of God and the love of God lived within me.

11.7   This is what you are now called to do:

11.8   Be aware that the love of God lives within you.
Live within the Peace of God.
Live by the truth.

11.9   This could be restated as you *are* love, you live *in* peace, you live *by* or in accord with the truth.

11.10   I have called the Kingdom of God the House of Truth rather than the House of Peace for a reason. What you are learning is no longer that the Kingdom of God or the House of Truth *exists*, but how to live within it. The question of how to live within it is best addressed by concentrating on living according to the truth.

11.11   While a lack of judgment has been stressed many times and we have adhered to the precept of not judging by denying any right or wrong, the difference between truth and illusion can no longer be denied. To realize the difference between truth and illusion is not to call one right and the other wrong but to simply recognize what they are. This is an important distinction that must be kept in mind as we proceed so that you are not tempted to judge those living in illusion or their reality.

Their reality does not exist. Believing in the reality of illusion will never make it the truth.

11.12   Thus we begin to address the temptations of the human experience.   Two are spoken of in tandem here.   The temptation to judge and the temptation to accept the existence of a reality other than the truth.

11.13   If I can tell you in truth that you are no different than I am, then you must see that you cannot begin to think of yourself as different than your brothers and sisters. *All* exist in the house of truth.   The house of illusion exists within the house of truth *because* it is where your brothers and sisters think they are. The house of illusion is not a *hell* to which anyone has been banished. It can at times be a chosen hell, just as it can at times, be a chosen heaven.   Choice, and the awareness of the power of choice that exists within, is all that differentiates one from the other.

11.14   You must not, however, see your brothers and sisters within the house of illusion, but must see them where they truly are — within the house of truth.   As soon as you would "see" the house of illusion, you would make it real, and with its reality, judgment would be upon you…not any judgment of God, but judgment of your own mind.

11.15   I remind you here that you are not being asked to *see* anything that is not the truth.   This is why the word *see* is consciously used here and why we now refrain from use of the word *perceive*. Perception is gone as soon as you truly see.

11.16   You will, of course, continue to be aware that very few realize that they exist in the house of truth. You will, in truth, for quite some time, be striving to remain aware even that you have changed dwelling places. There is a reason for this time of varying degrees of awareness. As the old continues to help you to learn lessons of the new, you will be seeing how the lessons of the illusion can be useful in a new way. Never forget that what was made for your use can serve in a new way and produce a new outcome. Do not be afraid to use anything available within the house of illusion to promote the recognition of truth. Do not be afraid of the house of illusion at all. What illusion can frighten those who know the truth?

11.17 This first lesson on the temptations of the human experience comes in truth as a warning against righteousness. It comes to remind you, as you replace the thought system of illusion with the thought system of the truth, that having remembered the truth of who you are, you are called to forget the personal self who would find this cause for righteousness. You are not right and others wrong. This temptation will not long be with you, for once the old thought system is thoroughly translated to the new, such ideas as right and wrong will be no more. It is only for this transitional phase that this, and all such reminders regarding the temptations of the human experience, are necessary.

chapter 12

the Physical Self in the House of Truth

12.1   Consciousness is a state of awareness. The statement "I am" is a statement of awareness of consciousness. Awareness preceded the statement of "I am." "I am" preceded the creation of the Self. The Self preceded the establishment of the personal self.

12.2   You exist within the *time* of consciousness of the personal self. Thus we begin our work with the personal self while also realizing that the personal self is a step in the chain of consciousness. The steps that came before that of the personal self did not come *within time*. The creation of *time* was simultaneous with the creation of the personal self. Because the steps that came before that of the personal self did not come within time, they are eternal; eternal levels of consciousness that still exist and have always existed.

12.3   Temptations of the human experience exist only in time. What we are about to do is move the human experience out of the realm of time. For this to happen, we must remove the temptations of the human experience of the personal self.

12.4   Matter and form are bound by time. Spirit is not. The house of truth cannot be bound by time and be a house of truth. How then can the personal self begin to realize the human experience outside of time? The answer is thus: by changing the consciousness of the personal self from a time-bound state of consciousness to an eternal state of consciousness. This change is the miracle. This miracle is the goal toward which we now work.

12.5   Realize that prior to this point our goal was returning to your awareness the truth of your identity. By changing our goal now, I am assuring you that you have become aware of the truth of your identity. The goal of this Course has been accomplished. Yet while your consciousness remains time-bound, your awareness is still limited. In order to remove the limits that continue to exist, we must remove all time-bound temptations.

12.6   These temptations are not temptations of the body. They may seem to be, but the body is neutral. All temptations originate in the mind and are but transferred to the body. Temptations do not originate from love. While some temptations will seem to be of love they are not.

12.7   As it dawns upon your once slumbering mind that change on a grand scale awaits, you will grow fearful if you do not realize that what is being proposed to you here is something completely new, something you have not even dreamed of. This state you have not even dared to dream of is a state in which only God's laws of love exist, even within the realm of physicality. What this means is that all that in this human experience has come of love will be retained. All that will be lost is what has come of fear.

12.8   Let's return a moment to the choice that was made for the human experience, the choice to express who you are in the realm of physicality. You were not "better" or more "right" before this choice was made than you are now. You made a choice consistent with the laws of creation and the steps of creation outlined above. From this choice, many experiences ensued. Some of these experiences were the result of fear, some the result of love. The choice to express who you are in physical terms was not a choice made of fear but made of love. A physical self is not inconsistent with the laws of God or of creation. It is simply a choice.

12.9   The life of the physical self became a life of suffering and strife only because the physical or personal self forgot that it exists in relationship and believed itself to be separate and alone. In its fear, it made an ego-self. Because the ego-self sprang from fear it was not consistent with the laws of love or of creation. Knowing it existed in a state inconsistent with the laws of God, it made of God a being to be feared, thus continuing and being unable to find release from the cycle of fear.

12.10   What would be a greater step in all of creation than a physical self able to choose to express the Self within the laws of love? A physical self able to express itself from within the house of truth in ways consistent with peace and love *is* the next step in creation, the rebirth of the Son of God known as the resurrection.

12.11   While this would seem to say that mistakes may occur within creation, remember that creation is about change and growth. There is no right or wrong within creation but there are stages of growth and change. Humankind is now passing through a tremendous stage of growth and change. Are you ready?

chapter 13

the Practice: No Loss But Only Gain

13.1   Now that we have established the consistency of our former purpose: establishing your identity, and our new purpose: the miracle that will allow you to exist as who you are in human form, we may proceed unencumbered by any doubt you might have had concerning whether or not you would desire the new goal toward which we work.

13.2   We proceed by further defining the temptations of the human experience. In *A Treatise on the Art of Thought*, we spoke of these temptations in regard to extremes of the human experience, saying that these extremes that draw you from the Peace of God, draw you from the state in which you are aware of who you are, and cause you to be aware only of a self of human experience or a personal self. While you may still feel a connection to God during such times, you will not be dwelling within the Peace of God. Your Self and God will be but memories to you while your reality remains that of the physical experience and the personal self. In such times you can conceive only of a God outside of yourself and trust not in the benevolence of the experience, whether it be an extreme experience of pain or of pleasure. You begin to fear that pleasure will end or that pain will not end. Once fear has entered, doubt and guilt are never far behind.

13.3   These temptations will concern you less and less as we uncover their true meaning by looking beyond the experiences themselves to the cause.

13.4   Broad brush-strokes have been made now, giving you the beginnings of a vision of a life in physical form that will not include the very temptations we are beginning to lay out. Because you have made these things that would but seem to tempt you, you have believed in them and their ability to affect you. You have unlearned many of these lessons and need not repeat unlearning that has been accomplished. The new learning that lies ahead of you now is simply learning in accordance with the new thought system of the truth, accepting the truth and leaving illusion behind. The new thought system is simple to learn. What is of love is truth. What is of fear is illusion. The temptation is to see love where it is not and to not see fear where it is. But your ability to distinguish between love and fear as cause is all that is important now as you will create the new according to what you believe to be the truth and translate into ideas.

13.5   Remember now that pleasure and pain, as perceived by the body, are from the same source. That source has not been the body, but your beliefs about your body and your self. You have believed pleasure to come at a cost, the cost of pain. You have believed in the laws of man, laws that were made to perpetuate the idea that you must pay for everything or earn everything that you would care to make your own, and then that you must protect what you have against those who would take it away.

13.6   This is a simple place to start because each of you is tempted to hang on to this idea despite all that it has cost you. To replace this idea with the idea of there being no loss but only gain under the laws of love, is to resist the temptation of requiring yourself to pay for what you gain.

13.7   I say this is a simple place to start because you can put this new idea into practice today and every day by simply refusing the temptation to believe in concepts such as earning and paying. How you implement this idea will be your choice. But the idea that you do not have to earn your way nor pay your way must be birthed and lived by. While most of you will immediately think of your survival needs, this is far from the only area in which the idea of earning or paying your way can be found. This old idea is consistent with all beliefs of an "if this then that" nature. You might start practicing this idea by repeating these words to yourself:

13.8   "I am safe and nothing that I do or do not do will threaten my safety."

13.9   As you say these words you will realize that you do believe in them. You believe, but you cannot *imagine* the truth of these words really being represented in the life you live here. This you must now do. You must represent the truth of these words with your life.

13.10   You are not, however, meant to test these words with foolish acts. To do so would be to act as if this were magic rather than the truth. To act as if this is the truth is what you are called to do. You may even begin with something as simple as choosing one thing a day that you will change to reflect the fact that you have accepted this new idea. Choose an act that will cause you no fear to begin with. For instance, you might tell yourself something such as this: "I have an idea that if I sleep as long as I feel I need to sleep in the morning, I will awaken refreshed and ready for my day and no dire consequences will befall me from this action." Another act might be as simple as allowing yourself to freely spend a small amount of money each day that you ordinarily would not spend, always with the *idea* in mind that this will not affect your budget in any negative respect.

13.11   While these examples may seem so simple that you regard them as little more than the self-help kind of advice I have said this course would not provide, they are but aids to help you in the development of your own ideas. If you remember that all of your ideas are to be based on love, you will not fail to birth ideas of consequence.

13.12   The second aspect of this lesson will then be regarding your ideas about the consequences that seem to result from whatever action your ideas have suggested. You must birth the idea of having no reason to fear these consequences, no matter what they may be. You must, in truth, birth the idea of benevolence and abundance.

13.13   Notice that the simple examples I gave were examples of action. Ideas can certainly be birthed without the need for action, but one of the factors that distinguishes an idea from a belief is a requirement of action. That action, while not necessarily physical, is the action of giving birth. Realize that you believe in many things that did not originate with your self. But it is not until you have your own ideas about those beliefs that you own those beliefs in terms of making them *your* beliefs. To believe without forming your own ideas about your beliefs is to be in danger of succumbing to false beliefs.

13.14   To form your own ideas is to be creative. Forming your own ideas happens in relationship. Taking action on your ideas forms a relationship between your physical form and your Self, as your physical self represents, in form, the thought or image produced within the Self. Ideas, in the context in which we are speaking of them here, are thoughts or images originating from the Self and being represented by the personal self. It is only in this way that the personal self will be able to represent the Self in truth.

chapter 14

Not Other Than Who You Are

14.1   The death of the ego thought system has made way for the birth of the thought system of the truth.   The thought system of the ego was based on fear. In this time of translation from one thought system to the other, the most subtle and yet significant change is the change from the foundation of fear: the basis of the ego thought system, to a foundation of love: the basis of the thought system of truth. While the foundation of fear, like the ego, will have left you now, a pattern of behaving fearfully may still remain and, as such, be a deterrent to new ideas and to action.   As long as these patterns of fear remain as   deterrents to action, you will not experience the freedom of *living* from the new thought system. The new thought system will still exist within your mind and heart, as nothing can now take this memory from you; but to experience the new thought system as thought alone will not bring about the changes you would so desire to have come about within your physical experience. You may live a more peaceful and meaningful life, but you will not become the savior I ask you to be, or the architects of the new world of heaven on earth that I call you to create.

14.2   Let me attempt to make the difference between having a new thought system and living by a new thought system more clear. Because you now are translating the thought system of the ego into the thought system of the truth, you will begin to *believe* in such things as benevolence and abundance. What this means is that you will slowly translate all ideas of scarcity into ideas of abundance, all ideas of blame into ideas of benevolence. Thus you might, after this period of translation, rather than cursing your station in life and feeling badly that

153

you do not enjoy the health, wealth, or stature of some others, accept your current status and begin to feel more peace and joy within it. If you are not well, you may cope more easily with your discomfort. If you are not financially secure, you may congratulate yourself on desiring less and be more content living a simple life. If you have felt a lack of respect, you may feel that what others think of you matters not and enjoy a heightened self-concept. While these would all be worthy aims they are not the goal toward which we work. These would be the consequences of new beliefs that are held but not lived. Soon these fragile states would be threatened by some situation or person, and judgment would return to label what is happening as "bad." A "god" outside of the self would soon be called upon to intercede. Blame would be placed. A return to equanimity would soon prevail, for those dwelling in the house of truth would not long abide with such illusions, but the pattern of the old would not be broken. Suffering and strife would still seem to be possible. You would merely look back after the interlude had passed and see the truth, realizing that a lesson had been learned and becoming aware that for a while you but flirted with illusion. This flirting with illusion is like unto the temptations of the human experience and would not occur were the temptations gone from you.

14.3   It should be becoming clear to you by now that although you now dwell in the house of truth you are capable of bringing with you old patterns of behavior. Once the translation from the old thought system to the new is complete, this will no longer happen. But the translation cannot be completed if you refuse to live by what you know...if you refuse to live as who you are.

14.4   You are quite capable of seeing the truth and still *acting* as if you see it not. This has been done for generation upon generation and may still happen if you do not heed these instructions.

14.5   I am, however, the bringer of Good News. Now I will repeat to you a piece of good news you may have forgotten: You would not be other than who you are. This is a key idea that will help you immeasurably in leaving behind patterns of behavior based on the old thought system of fear. Despite the foundation of fear upon which your old thought system was based, you still would not be other than who you are. What this means to the learning stage you are at now is that you but think you are discontent with much of your life. As you begin to dwell in the house of truth and see with the eyes of love, you will see far less about the life you lead that you would change than you would imagine. You fear where all your new ideas might take you, and for some great changes may surely await. Yet those who will be visited by great change are but those who desire it, and even these will find that great changes will not cause them to be other than who they are. There is nothing wrong with who you are!

14.6   As you see newly with the eyes of love, you will be much more likely to see love everywhere within the life you currently live than to see the need to change your life completely in order to find love! You who are worried about the risks you may be required to take, worry not! The changes that come to you will be chosen changes. You will lose nothing you would keep.

14.7   This is precisely why you must choose not to keep the life of discomfort caused by perceived illness, the life of scarcity caused by perceived lack, the lack of stature caused by perceived disrespect. It is only by your choice that you will keep these things and only by your choice that these things will leave you.

14.8   It is only your old uncertainty that will make you fear the matter of choice that lies before you. This choice is not the choice of continuous decision making but simply the choice to live by the truth of the new thought system. If you but let go the old, and with it the patterns of behavior caused by fear, the new will reveal to you all that you would keep and all that you would leave behind. What you would keep is of love. What you would leave behind is of illusion.

14.9   You will clearly see all of the choices that throughout your life have been made in love and made of you a person you would not be other than. You will also clearly see all of the choices that throughout your life were caused by fear and how little consequence they had in truth. These fearful choices took nothing from you nor from others.

14.10   If there are things that you, at this point, still hold to yourself and call unforgivable, now is the time to let them go. If you have read the paragraph above and feel it is fine for some others not to regret their choices but not for you, I ask you to trust in my assurance that this is not so. You must choose to leave this blaming of yourself behind, no matter what it is for which you feel you have need to blame yourself. You would not be here if you had not already felt regret and sorrow for the hurts you have caused others. Whatever actions you have not previously brought to love to be seen in a new light, are now revealed in the light of truth.

14.11   We have spoken already of historical causes for vengeance and blame. The suffering that has been chosen has been mighty. The choice now is not a choice to explore the why behind it or to look for remedies for the past. The choice now is whether you want suffering to continue or want to abolish it for all time. If you are holding onto regrets you are holding on to blame. If you are holding onto blame you are holding onto bitterness. If these regrets and blame have to do with your self you may not feel as if you have the right to let them go. If you do not feel as if you have the right to let them go, you are choosing to remain embittered and choosing to be punished for your "sins." While this is what you continue to choose, this is what will continue to be evidenced in your world. This is the only act you can choose worthy of being called selfishness. Be self "less" rather than selfish now and allow the self that you would blame to pass away into the illusion from which it came. Remember that bitterness, like the ego, has existed in all. If your brother or sister would not give up bitterness in order to usher in a world of peace, would you not think this a selfish act?

14.12 Atonement, or correction, is not of you but of God. You might think of this in terms of nature and look upon nature's ability to correct itself. You are a part of nature. Your body can correct or heal itself, and so can your mind and heart...if they are allowed to do so. A time-bound consciousness that hangs onto the past as if it were the truth, does not allow correction to take place. The past is no more and neither the present nor the future can be built upon it. This is why we have spent so much time unlearning and why we continue with lessons of forgetting.

14.13 Resurrection or rebirth must be total to be at all. Can you not see why you cannot hang onto the past? The new cannot have historical precedents. This is why you have been assured that what you are called to is a life so new that you cannot even imagine it. Imagine not the past and make for yourself no cause to prolong it. The past is but a starting point for the future. Just as we talked of the consequences of blame and how you are unaware of all that proceeds from the idea of blame, so too is it with the past. Like a story yet to be written, that which follows the first page will be based upon the first page.

14.14 We are writing a new first page, a new Genesis. It begins now. It begins with the rebirth of a Self of love. It begins with the birth of Christ in you and in your willingness to live in the world as the Christ-Self.

chapter 15

the New Beginning

15.1 Some of you have had more experience with new beginnings than others. For most mature adults, some form of new beginning has taken place or been offered. Those within the relationship of marriage have often had occasion to choose to forgive the past and to begin again to build a new relationship. Others, in a similar relationship, might have chosen to let the past go and enter into new relationships. Parents have welcomed home errant children to give them the chance to begin again. At all stages of life new friendships are formed and the relationship with each new friend provides for a new beginning. Some begin anew through changes in locale and employment. Each new school year of the young provides a fresh start. Deaths of loved ones and the births of new family members form new configurations in a life. Nature begins anew each spring.

15.2 What hampers new beginnings of all kinds within the human experience are ideas that things cannot be different than they once were. The only true departure from this idea has concerned the occasions of birth and death. This is something we will return to, but first let us look at other types of new beginnings and all that would hamper them from taking place.

15.3 New beginnings do not occur outside of relationship. The idea of special relationship is one that hampers new beginnings. Special relationships of all types are based upon expectations — expectations of certain behavior — and expectations of continued special treatment within the relationship. Even, and sometimes especially, what is considered poor behavior can come to be an expectation difficult to deviate from within the special relationship. But whether the expectation is of special treatment or poor behavior matters not. It is the expectation of a "known" set of criteria concerning the relationship, a set of criteria based upon the past, that is most often what prevents new beginnings from truly being new.

15.4   Often new beginnings are offered or considered "in spite of" circumstances of the past that would seem to make them foolish. There is always something that is expected to change. This idea is countered internally by the idea that at some basic level, human beings do not change. You cannot imagine those you are in relationship with being other than who they are. This is consistent with the truth. Who anyone is, however, is not contingent upon who they have represented themselves to be in the past.

15.5   When attempting to give oneself or another a new beginning, you often act "as if" you believe a new beginning is possible, even while awaiting the lapse that will surely prove to you that the new beginning is but an act and that nothing has really changed. A student who failed to learn the prior year, while eager and confident in being able to succeed in the current year, will continue to be plagued by memories of failure. The alcoholic can approach each day with faith while keeping fresh memories of past abuse or humiliation in the hopes that they will discourage a repeat of the old behavior. The loved one of an alcoholic can similarly approach each day with faith even while suspiciously looking for signs that faith is unwarranted. The criminal is not expected to be rehabilitated despite the efforts of the system and the hopes of their loved ones.

15.6   Everyone believes they carry the baggage of the past, not only their own but that of all the special relationships in which they have been involved. To have a special relationship with someone who has failed at offered new beginnings becomes a failure for all involved. Each sets their own criteria for success or failure and their own timing for the accomplishment of the same. Some would see six months of change as the basis for trust in the new. For others six years would not be enough.

15.7   You must now birth the idea that human beings do indeed change. While you have known instinctively that there is a core, a center to each that is unchangeable, you must now give up the idea that this core or center has been represented by the past. You must forget the idea that the future cannot be different than the past.

15.8   With the death of the ego, special relationships too have breathed their last. As I said before, these will but seem to be remedial lessons. What they are, in truth, are aids to help you birth the new ideas that will break the patterns of old.

15.9   The new beginning you are called to now is a new beginning that, like all the others you have offered or attempted, will take place in relationship. The difference is that this new beginning will take place in holy, rather than special, relationship.

15.10   The holy relationship has been accomplished by the joining of the mind and heart in unity. The holy relationship is with the Self, the Self that abides in unity with all within the house of truth. This relationship makes the Self one with all and so brings the holiness of the Self to all.

15.11   There are no impediments to this new beginning save for the finalizing of the translation of the thought system of the ego to the thought system of the truth. It is impossible to learn the new with the thought system of the old; it is impossible to learn the truth through the same methods that have been used in the past to learn illusion. This Course teaches that love cannot be learned. I have said here that love, peace, and truth are interchangeable ideas within the new thought system. Truth, like love, is not something that you can learn. The good news is that you have no need to learn the truth. The truth exists within you and you are now aware of its reality.

15.12 How then, do you access and live within this new reality, this new beginning? Through living by the truth.

15.13 These treatises are no longer concerned with course work as the work of this course has been accomplished in you. These treatises are simply concerned with assisting you with living what you have learned. Learning was needed in order to return you to your Self. Despite whatever method you feel you used to learn what you have learned, what this course did was by-pass the way of learning of the ego and call upon the Christ in you to learn anew. That learning put an end to the old. Living what you have learned will usher in the new.

15.14 These examples of your former ideas about new beginnings have simply been used to demonstrate why you cannot approach this new beginning as you have those of the past. What will assist you most as the translation of the old thought system for the new continues are the beliefs that you adopted with the assistance of the Treatise on Unity:

15.15 You are accomplished.
Giving and receiving are one in truth.
There is no loss but only gain within the laws of love.
Special relationships have been replaced by holy relationship.

15.16 What we are adding now to these beliefs is the idea that these beliefs can be represented in form. These beliefs can, with the help of the new thought system, change the very nature of the self described by the words *human being*. This calls for still more forgetting as you must consciously let go of all of

161

your ideas of the limitations inherent in your concept of what it means to be a human being.

15.17   While you would not be other than who you are, who you are is not limited to the concept of human being nor to the laws of man. If you continue to act as if you are still the same being that you have represented yourself to be in the past, you will not be living by the truth but by illusion.

15.18   Illusion is the "truth" by which you have lived. The total replacement of illusion with the truth is what the new thought system will accomplish. Obviously, this replacement must be total. The means for making this total replacement are in your hands but you are hardly empty-handed. The truth goes with you as does the love and peace of God.

chapter 16

Willingness, Temptation, and Belief

16.1   Willingness to live by the truth is the only offering you are asked to make to God. You need make no other offerings. No sacrifices need be made and sacrifices are, in truth, unacceptable to God. You are asked to give up nothing but unwillingness.

16.2   Saying that willingness is the only offering that is required of you is the same as saying that you do not need to, and in truth cannot, give anything else or anything less. You do not need to give your effort to this calling. You do not need to struggle to create the new world you are called to create. You do not need to have a plan, and you do not need to know precisely what this new world will look like. You simply need to be willing to live by the truth.

16.3   You must forget the idea that you can create the new from the old. If this were possible, you would indeed be called to effort and to struggle, to planning and to a state of knowing that for which it is you plan. These have been the ways of creation in the thought system of the ego, ways that have brought much advancement to the forms you occupy without changing their nature in the slightest measure. All the effort of the ego has not brought an end to suffering or strife, nor made of this illusion a happy dream.

16.4   Although you may still feel confused and lacking in ability to do what I am asking of you, I feel confident in also saying that you are more content and happy, more peaceful, and more free of fear than you have ever been. While your life may not have changed in ways that you would like, and while its limitations may seem even more frustrating than before, I am also confident in saying that a hope has been instilled within you, a hope for the very changes that you feel you need in order to reflect, within your daily life, the new Self you have become.

16.5   We spoke once before within *A Course of Love* of your impatience and of this course acting as a trigger that would release all such impatience for what will be. Impatience for what will be can only be satisfied by what is.

16.6   What is, *is*, despite the lag in time that would seem to make all that we speak of here a blueprint for some future reality. All that would keep this lag in time a constant, and make it seem as if what is now is still awaiting replacement by what will be, is a change that must occur within. This change has to do with the time-bound temptations of the human experience. All of these temptations relate to the beliefs set forth in the Treatise on Unity.

16.7   *You are already accomplished.*

16.8   By saying that you are not only accomplished but The Accomplished, it is being said that you are already what you have sought to be. Thus in order to live by the truth, you must live in the world as The Accomplished and cease struggling to be other than who you are in truth. This struggling to be other than who you are in truth is a temptation of the human experience. This temptation will come in many forms, all of which will be related to an old pattern of dissatisfaction with yourself. It will be related to the intrigue of the challenge and actually be couched in patterns that have you attempting to "accomplish" set goals in life. The key to resisting this temptation is not resistance at all but the idea that you are already accomplished. Keeping this idea in the forefront of your mind and heart will aid the translation of this aspect of the ego thought system to the thought system of the truth.

16.9   *Giving and Receiving are One in Truth.*

16.10   By saying that giving and receiving are one in truth it is being said that you are lacking only in what you do not give. The belief in lack is a temptation of the human experience. This temptation will relate to all situations in which you feel you have something to gain from some "other." Again, this will be related to old patterns of dissatisfaction with the self. It has to do with any ideas you may still hold concerning others having more than you have or to desires that you may feel have gone unfulfilled. While you may think that this means you are being asked to do without, this is not the case. You are simply being asked to give that you might receive and to receive that you might give.

16.11   *There is no Loss but only Gain within the Laws of Love.*

16.12   By saying that there is no loss but only gain within the laws of love, you are being told to have no fear. Fear of loss is a great temptation of the human experience. If it were not for this fear of loss, you would not find it difficult to live by the thought system of the truth. This temptation relates very strongly to your ideas of change and as such is the greatest detriment to your new beginning. This temptation relates to everything you fear to do because of the consequences your actions might bring. These fears rob you of your certainty and result in a lack of trust. The key to resisting this temptation is not resistance at all but the idea that there is no loss but only gain within the laws of love.

16.13   *Special Relationships have been replaced by Holy Relationship.*

16.14   By saying that special relationships have been replaced by holy relationship, it is being said that your only relationship is with the truth and that you no longer have a relationship with illusion.   Your fears in regard to special relationships are a temptation of the human experience.   This temptation will relate to any issues you consider to be issues of relationship. All of your desires, fears, hopes and expectations of others are temptations that arise from your old idea of special relationships.   All of your plans to do good and be good, to help others, and to struggle to make the world a better place, fall into this category.   Your notions of wanting to protect or control are also notions based upon the necessity you have felt for the continuation of special relationships.

16.15   Now you must forget the idea of needing to maintain specialness.   A key aid in helping you to put this temptation behind you is the idea of the holy relationship in which all exist in unity and within the protection of love's embrace.   If you but live by the idea that representing who you are in truth will create a new heaven on earth, you can lay aside any fears that others will suffer due to the changes your new Self will create. As you live with awareness of the love of God within you, you will see that you have no need for special love relationships. You will realize that the love and the Self you now have available to share in relationship are all that you would share in truth.   You will recognize that no others have a need for you to make them special, for you will see the truth of who they are rather than the illusion of who you would have them be.

16.16   All of these temptations worked together in the thought system of the ego and created patterns that caused them to but seem to be intertwined and all encompassing.   Nothing but the truth is all encompassing.   Illusion is made of parts that do not form real connections but that only seem to have the ability to build upon each other.   Let one part go and soon all the remaining parts will crumble into the dust from which they came. The cement that was used to hold together the house of illusion was only your fear.

16.17 Accept one part or tenet of the truth and see the reverse take place. See how quickly the thought system of the truth builds upon itself and forms a real and true interrelated whole. What forms the house of truth is love eternal and it has always encompassed you, even unto encompassing the house of illusion that you made to obscure it from yourself.

chapter 17

A Mistake in Learning

17.1   Why would you ever have chosen to obscure the truth? As we have already shown, to have chosen to express the Self in physical form was a choice consistent with the laws of love. There was no need for the Self to be separate in order for this to be so, but there was a need for the Self to have an observable form and to exist in relationship with others with observable forms. This was simply so that expressions of love could be created and observed within the realm of physicality.

17.2   The biblical story of Adam and Eve that has them eating from the tree of knowledge is an illustration of the effect of observation and the judgment that sprang from it. The self "fell" from unity through judgment of what it observed as being "other than" itself — through making distinctions between the self and all in creation that existed with the self. This is why the story of creation includes the naming of creatures. It was the beginning of perception and of the idea that what was observable was "other than" he who did the observing.   Now your science is proving to you the relationship between the observer and the observed, the effect that one cannot help but have upon the other. Science still has a long way to go in determining through its processes what this says about the nature of man but it is closer every day to understanding the unity and interconnectedness of all things.

17.3   As soon as spirit took on form, man began to exist in time because there became a need for a beginning and an ending to the chosen experience. Each self of form is born *into* time and each self of form dies *out* of time.   Both birth and death have always existed as choices, as beginnings and endings to the finite experience of time. It is the nature of what is finite to begin and end. Birth and death are all you have seen as true new beginnings.

17.4   Time is a measurement of the "time" it takes for learning to occur. A *new* experience was chosen — the experience of existing within the realm of physicality. As such, it was as much a new beginning as the new beginning you are now called to. It required the learning of a new thought system, the thought system of the physical, a thought system that was not needed before there was physical form. The creation story of Adam and Eve, as well as many other creation stories, but tell of a "mistake" in the learning of a thought system of physicality, a mistake that became a building block for all that came after it.

17.5   That mistake was seeing God as "other than" and separate from the self. While it was important to the desired experience to learn the lessons of what was observable within the physical realm, to have begun to forget the unobservable began a process of unlearning or forgetting of the truth that has led, through the learning of untruth in the mechanism of time, to the world in which you now exist. It may seem ridiculous to say that the untrue can be learned, but this is exactly what has been learned during the time of your experience in physical form. Since your true Self could not learn the untrue, a new self, which we have called the ego self, was made. Since the ego self cannot learn the true, your true Self had to be appealed to for this learning to take place.

17.6   The Holy Spirit was called upon to return this remembrance to minds and hearts. But again let me remind you that the Holy Spirit is not other than who you are but an aspect of who you are and Who God Is. Let me remind you also that names, such as *Holy Spirit*, are but word symbols that represent what is. So think now of whatever stories you know of the Holy Spirit, stories that symbolize what is. In these stories, the Holy Spirit is always called upon to return the true Self to the self of illusion. The *holy spirit* is called to return to your mind and heart.

17.7   You were told in *A Treatise on the Art of Thought* that the time of the Holy Spirit has ended and the time of the second coming of Christ is here. The name of Christ was associated with my name, the name Jesus, because I lived as a man with the *holy spirit* in my mind and heart, and as such represented the truth. Many others by many other names have represented the truth and in so doing dispelled illusion within themselves and those who followed their teachings and example. This has occurred within the time of the Holy Spirit.

17.8   The Holy Spirit, unlike God the Creator, has known the existence of the illusion and the thought system of the ego-self and been able to communicate within that illusion. Without this means of communication with the ego-self, the ability to learn the truth could not have returned to you. The time of the Holy Spirit has now ended because the time of illusion is now called to an end. What is finite has an end point and this is that end point for the time of illusion. The return of Christ, or *your* ability and willingness to live as your true Self, to live in the house of truth rather than the house of illusion, is what will end the time of illusion. Just as the truth is the truth, and illusion is illusion — just as these things are what they are without judgment, so is the beginning the beginning and the end the end. The beginning we speak of here is the same as the end we speak of here. The *time* of the Holy Spirit, or the time in which communication was needed between the illusion and the truth, *must* end in order for the truth to become the one reality.

chapter 18

Observation

18.1   You may wonder rightly then, how those who have not learned by the Holy Spirit will learn. They will now learn through observation.

18.2   Let us return now to the concept of observation and link it with ideas as we have spoken of them here. Observation, the ability to observe what the Self expresses, was part of the original choice for physical form. The word *observance* has rightly been linked with divine worship and devotion. Minds that have been unwilling to accept or learn an unobservable truth, will now accept and learn from observable truth. This is why you must *become* that observable truth.

18.3   Observance happens in relationship, the very relationship that disallowed the making of a separate self. Observance is linked to cause and effect being one. What is observed is in relationship with the observer and this relationship causes an effect. Because this was part of the original choice for the physical experience, it is a natural choice to serve our new purpose of the miracle that will allow you to exist as who you are in human form. See what perfect sense this makes, as your human form is an observable form. It is thus from observable form that the final learning will take place. This is the perfect example of using what you have made for a new purpose. It is the perfect ending for the desired experience as it was the goal of the desired experience.

18.4   Expressing who you are in physical form will return remembrance to the minds of *those who observe* your expression.

Further, *your observance* of your brothers and sisters will return remembrance to their minds and hearts. It is, in fact, your observance of the truth of your brothers and sisters that is the miracle we have stated as our new goal.

18.5   I repeat, your observance of the truth of your brothers and sisters *is* the miracle.

18.6   If you observe health rather than disease, abundance rather than poverty, peace rather than conflict, happiness rather than sadness — disease poverty, conflict, and sadness will be no more real to your brothers and sisters than it is to you.

18.7   A mind and heart joined in unity observes the truth where once a mind and heart separated by illusion observed illusion.

18.8   It will seem at first as if you are asked to deny the facts that you see before you in order to observe something other than what is there. You must constantly remember that your observance is now an act of worship and of devotion and that you are called to observe the truth rather than illusion no matter how real illusion may still seem to be.

18.9   In this way, you will join the mechanisms of your physical form to the new thought system of the truth. Your body is a neutral form that will but serve you in the manner in which you choose to have it serve you. It has always been led by your thought system. If it is no longer instructed by the thought system of illusion, it is natural that it will now be instructed by the thought system of the truth. Thus your eyes will learn to observe only the truth, even unto seeing what before but seemed unobservable.

18.10   We also now link observance and ideas. Ideas form in the mind. You are used to thinking that what you observe forms outside of your mind. This is the thinking of the ego-thought system. The thought system of the truth realizes that the external world is but a reflection of the internal world. You can observe with your eyes closed as easily as you can observe with your eyes open. You can *observe* by having an idea of another's health, abundance, peace, and happiness. You can observe this within yourself because it exists within your Self. What exists within you is shared by all. This is the relationship of the truth that unites all things and that must now become observable.

chapter 19

Physical Reality

19.1   You must not fear the changes that will occur within your physical form as it begins to be guided by the thought system of the truth rather than the thought system of illusion. You will fear these changes less if you realize that all that has come of love will be kept and that all that has come of fear will fall away. You have, in other words, no need to fear that the end of the special relationship will separate you from your loved ones. You have no need to fear that the joys you have shared with others will be no more. You have no more need to fear the loss of physical joys than you have to fear the loss of mental and spiritual joys.

19.2   For ages man has thought that spiritual joy diminishes physical joy. While there is no physical joy that is limited to the physical — no joy felt by the physical form alone — the joy that comes of things physical can certainly still be experienced and expressed. This is no call for judgment upon the physical. How could this be true when the physical is now called upon to serve the greatest learning man has ever known?

19.3   Put these fears to rest.

19.4   For ages, physical reality has been linked to temptations of the human experience. Let us now dispel this link. The physical form has been blamed for choices made from lust and greed, hate and fear, vengeance and retribution. These things have always had as their cause the thought system of the ego or the bitterness of the heart. As cause and effect are one, there is no effect that has been seen in physical form that has not had a

174

corresponding cause birthed in the ego thought system or the bitterness of the heart.

19.5   That these feelings can be "acted out" by the body, and in the acting out cause harm to other bodies, is the cause for blame and fear of the body.   So too is it with actions linked with survival needs.

19.6   For ages the survival needs of the body have gone unquestioned and been held paramount. The *will* of the body to survive has been blamed for all actions that have arisen from real and perceived lack.   Yet the body has no *will* and the survival of the true Self is not based upon it.

19.7   Because the spiritual life has so often been linked with celibacy I will mention sexual union specifically here to put behind you any fear that you may have that an end to sexual union may be called for. While some of you may have less desire for physical joining as you become more aware of unity, some may have more desire for physical joining as an expression of that union.   Neither option is reason for judgment.

19.8   There is only one distinction that need be made: what comes of love and what comes of fear. All expressions of love are of maximal benefit to everyone.   While you may, for a while, not see that all that are not expressions of love are expression of fear, I assure you that this is the case.   Any behavior, including sexual behavior, that is not of love, is of fear. All that comes of fear is nothing. What this means is that cause and effect are not influenced by what comes of fear. You may still think that suffering and "bad" behavior have had great effects but they have not.   At times the love that is received following suffering, or that may seem to arrive due to the reason of some affliction may be seen as having been gained by lessons learned from suffering or affliction; but this is no more the case than it was the case in regard to our discussion of extremes.

19.9   There is no longer any *time* to waste on such illusions. The thought system of the truth sees no value in suffering and so sees it not in truth. The thought system of the truth is a thought system that is not split by varying goals and desires. It is a thought system of unity. It is a thought system of one thought, one goal. That goal is the original thought that began the experience in physical form, the thought of expressing the Self in observable form.

19.10   Leave all blaming of the body behind and see it not as the source of temptations of the human experience. The true source of these temptations has been revealed to lie within the faulty beliefs to which the body merely responded. The body's response to the new thought system will be different in many ways, none of which will lead you to feel that you have lost anything of value to you.

19.11   While others still remain tied to the old thought system, human behavior will still reflect harmful actions that will seem to arise from bodily temptations. Although you will now represent who you are in physical form in a new way, you can still see that your actions of the past but represented who you believed yourself to be. Those continuing to express themselves in harmful ways are deeply entrenched in false beliefs about themselves. Because they are not expressing who they are, their expressions are meaningless and have no effect *in truth* but only *in illusion*. To live *in truth* is to live without fear of the meaningless acts of those living *in illusion* because they will be unable to cause effect in the house of truth.

19.12   These lessons could not be taught while blame remained within your thought system. No victim is to blame for the violence done to them or sick person to blame for the illness within them. But you must be able to look at and see reality for what it is. Just as we are telling you that new beliefs and ideas will lead to a new reality, old beliefs and ideas led to the old reality, a reality that will still exist for some even after it changes completely for you.

19.13 This will seem even more inconsistent with a benevolent universe than it once did because of the difference between one reality and the other, a difference that couldn't be seen until it was represented in an observable manner, something you will now do.

19.14 You would think that this disparity would be divisive, extremely uncomfortable, and even rage producing for those still living in illusion. But it will be much more tempting to be divisive, uncomfortable, and rage producing for those living in the new. Many who observe the new from the house of illusion will still be able to deny what they see. Just think of how many saints and miracles you have heard of in the past without being moved to believe that they mean anything at all about the nature of who *you* are. This is why no more time can be wasted and why so many are being called in the strongest manner it is possible to call them. It is only when what is observable is so widely evident that it can no longer be denied that changes on a large scale will begin to be seen.

19.15 You will be tempted to return to the house of illusion to gather those within and bid them join you in the reality of the truth. But in this time of Christ, a *new* time, a time without parallel or comparison, this will not be possible. It has been said from the beginning that your role will not be to evangelize or to be convincing. You cannot argue the case of truth in the courtroom of illusion.

19.16 While this would seem to leave some without hope, it will leave no one without choice. It will make the one clear and only choice evident. It is a choice to live in truth or in illusion. There are many ways that can still be found to come to the truth. One or another *way* of getting to the truth will become so attractive that few will be able to resist. What will make this choice so attractive will not be martyrs and saintly souls stricken with every calamity and yet remaining to tell those who would listen about the glory of God. What will make this choice so attractive are ordinary people living extraordinary, and miraculous, and observable lives.

chapter 20

Suffering and Observance

20.1   By saying that there is no longer any time to be wasted on illusion we are saying that you will no longer serve time but that time will serve you. Time *was* wasted on illusion and so but seemed to become a master that made of you a slave. Now time must be thought of in a new way, a way that has to do with effectiveness. Illusion has at its base a false cause and so no effects that exist in truth. Now your every thought and action will have effect and the choices that lie before you will be choices of where your thoughts and actions will have the *greatest* effect.

20.2   Although there was no sense to be made of concepts such as *more or less* within illusion, and although *more or less* are concepts also foreign to the truth, there is sense to be made from these concepts in regards to the *learning* of the truth. As this is all that time is for, and all that time is but a measurement of, it rightly follows that learning can take place at a slow pace or a fast pace. There is no more or less to learning in terms of knowing the truth that you have always known, but there are degrees of remembering and since this is what we work to have occur, time can become our ally by using it for effectiveness.

20.3   Again, do not let your thoughts stray to benefiting and effecting others. In unity, all others are one with you. What you strive for in effectiveness is your own learning. Now, rather than learning the truth, you are learning how to live by the truth. This will benefit you and in so doing benefit all others.

20.4   In *A Treatise on the Art of Thought*, you were asked to request a miracle as a learning device. This learning device had two aspects. The first was to reveal to you your fears concerning the miracle so that you would learn from them. The second was to assure you that the miracle is the most effective way of convincing you of who you are.

20.5   Let us now link observation and the miracle. An easy illustration is provided, as so often is the case, by looking at observation under the guidance of the ego-thought system, thus seeing the errors of the old way in order to realize the perfect sense of the new.

20.6   Think about a situation in which you have observed the illness or suffering of another. Sympathy is the most common observance in such a circumstance. You might feel called to tears, to words that acknowledge how "bad" the illness or suffering is. You are likely to be drawn into discussions concerning how the illness or suffering can be "fought." You are likely to hear questions concerning why the illness or suffering has come to be and to hear or offer comments about the unfairness of the situation. Judgment is never far from these observations. Suffering, you would think, could not be seen as anything but "bad." You cannot feel anything but "sorry" for the one suffering. Yet you are always drawn, despite these feelings of the "badness" of the situation, to offer encouragement. If the situation is particularly grim — and realize that this too is a judgment, for some illnesses and suffering are surely seen as being worse than others — encouragement is given despite the "fact" that it is unwarranted. Even while you offer encouragement, you worry about giving "false" hope and wonder how realistic you should be or should assume the other to be. You look ahead, and in your mind's eye you "observe" the future as a repetition of the present or as a long war with little chance of being won. You chide yourself not to deny the facts, and you begin, along with the one whom you observe, the long walk toward death's door.

All of these actions could be called your "observance" of the situation.

20.7   You do not seem to realize that all of this is happening in relationship and that the relationship is meaningful or able to cause effect. You can't imagine not feeling "bad" given such circumstances. You cannot imagine not offering sympathy. You think it naive to believe in positive outcomes. You listen to statistics of what has occurred before and in similar situations, and you believe in what the statistics would seem to tell you. You might "thank God" for technology that would seem to offer hope, or for drugs that would ease suffering, and you might pray that God spare this one from a future seemingly already written, and think that is more realistic and even helpful than living by the laws of truth.

20.8   You will see it as quite difficult at first to respond to such situations in a new way, but all situations within the house of illusion call for the same response, the response of love to love. Why think you it is loving to believe in suffering? Do you not begin to see that in so doing you but reinforce it? What you might even call the "fact" of it? Can you not instead ask yourself what harm could be done by offering a new kind of observance?

20.9   While you need not act in ways inconsistent with compassion or even verbalize your new beliefs, you are being told directly here that no circumstance should call you to abandon them.

20.10   Your new thought system is not tied to beliefs of an *if this, then that* nature. Look at the examples all around you. People who live what you call healthy lives succumb to illnesses and accidents just as do those who live what you call unhealthy lives. "Good" people have as much calamity befall them as do "bad." I am not calling you to just another version of being good or mentally healthy, to exercises in visualization or positive thinking. I am calling you to live by the truth and to never deny it. To see no circumstance as cause to abandon it. Yes, I am providing you with means to help you know how to live by the truth, but the means are never to be confused with outcome. Your observance is to remain with cause rather than stray to effect.

20.11 Miracles are not about the end result but are merely the means of living by the truth. Miracles are not meant to be called upon to create specific outcomes in specific circumstances. Miracles are meant to be lived by, as the truth is meant to be lived by. Not because you desire an outcome, but because it is who you are and because you realize you can no longer be, live, or think as other than who you are in truth. This is how thorough your learning must be. It is a learning that must not change to fit the circumstances of illusion but be unchanging to fit the circumstances of the truth.

20.12 As has been said before you can no longer return to the house of illusion, not even to cause explosions within it. You have stepped out of this house and are called not to return. To turn your back not on the truth nor on God nor love.

20.13 Will those you love still suffer? Many may. But not with your help. Will many more, with your help, see an end to suffering? Many will. Will an end to suffering be what you work toward? No. This is not your work. This is not about your effort. This is about your observance; your observance of the laws of love. Your observance is to remain with cause rather than to stray to effect, the manner of living practiced by those who have birthed the idea that cause and effect are one in truth.

20.14 I thank you for your strong desire to be saviors of the world and to end her suffering. I thank you for your compassion and for your desire to be of service to the world. But I call to you from peace and ask for you to remain in peace

182

with me and let not the suffering of the world call you from it. When these things of the world threaten to call you from your peace, you must remind yourself that it is only from within the Peace of God that your wholeheartedness and our unity is accomplished.

20.15   My dear brothers and sisters in Christ, let nothing call you to return to the ways of old.   They do not work!   To minister to those within the house of illusion is to offer the temporary to the temporary when I call you to offer the eternal to the eternal.   The new way will work wherever it finds willingness.   You cannot call others to abandon their willingness to live in illusion by joining them there!   You can only call others to a willingness to set illusion aside and to begin the journey home to unity.   You can only call to them from unity if you are already there!

20.16   These calls go out from love to love.   It is not the words of your mouth that will be heard or the language of your mind that will be responded to.   It is the love within your heart that will sound the call.   And when it is heard and your brother or sister reaches out to you, all you need but ask for is a little willingness.   All you need do is open the door through which love can enter.

20.17   And thus we return to observance, the observance of love by love. See not what love would not have you see. Turn from the dark ways of illusion and shine the light of truth for all to see. Remain who you are and continue to live by the laws of love in every circumstance, and you bring love to every circumstance.   Be not dismayed nor discouraged by those who do not see and have no willingness to offer.   Just know these aren't the ones given you to bring to love and trust that none will remain forever lost to his or her own Self.

20.18   You are as pioneers to this new world.   Its mere existence will attract others and each will find the price of admission is their willingness to leave the old behind. This is a price they must freely give and it cannot be extorted from them, not from special ones of your choosing, and not from anyone. You are released from a burden never meant to rest upon you even if it is one you might have freely chosen. Your task is to create the new world and make it observable, not for you to recruit others to it.

20.19 The circumstance of suffering or illness is not different but the same as every other circumstance you will encounter. You will encounter truth or illusion and nothing else for there is nothing else. There is but one call for all circumstances, the call to love from love, the call that welcomes all to live in truth.

chapter 21

the Identity of the True Self

21.1   The truth is not a set of facts. Written truth is not the truth but only the arrangement of the truth into language. You have a birth certificate that states the truth about your birth. The birth certificate is not the truth but symbolic of the truth.

21.2   The truth is not symbolic. It is. It is the same for everyone.

21.3   There are no two sides to the truth. There is not more than one truth. There is one truth.

21.4   The truth is not a concept. It is real. It is *all* that is real.

21.5   Your real Self exists in truth. It does not exist in illusion.

21.6   Your personal self exists in illusion. It is called a personal self because it is attached to a person. A person is a being born into time, a being whose existence began in time and will end in time.

21.7   The only means for the personal self and the true Self to exist together is for the truth to be lived in time. In order for the truth to be lived in time you must forget your uncertainty and be certain of the truth.

21.8   This certainty is antithetical to you. You think that to believe in one truth is to deny other truths. There is only one truth. Untruth *must* now be denied.

21.9   This will sound intolerant to you. It *is* a stance intolerant of illusion. You must no longer see illusion for it is no longer there! This is how you must live with it. You must live with it as you once lived with the truth. You must find it unobservable! It must become a concept only. Illusion is a set of facts, or in other words, a set of information. These facts are subject to change and mean one thing to one person and one thing to another. Illusion is symbolic. And what's more it symbolizes nothing for it does not symbolize what is!

21.10   This is your conundrum. When you have never known what *is* you have never been able to be certain. You have no *experience* with certainty other than...and this is a crucial other than...your certainty of your own identity, the very identity this course has disproved. This identity has been seen as your personal self. Thus your personal self is the only place in which you have experience that can now be used for a new purpose.

21.11   Even while this experience is experience of an ego-self it is still an experience as near to certainty as you have been capable simply because you could not exist without an identity. You might think of this as being certain of facts and information, for these are the things about yourself that few of you have doubted. Those who have had cause to doubt the circumstances of their birth are often consumed with a desire to discover these unknown circumstances. For it is your birth, your name, the history of your family and the accumulated experiences of your lifetime, that are the things upon which you draw to feel the certainty you feel about your personal self. You identify yourself as male or female, married or single, homosexual or heterosexual. You might call yourselves Chinese or Lebanese or American, black or white or Indian. Your personal self may be deeply affected by these things you call yourself or may be minimally affected.

21.12   And even more so than these things, although this hasn't as often been considered as part of what makes you certain of your personal self, are the thoughts of your mind, thoughts that while certainly changeable, are unmistakably claimed to be your own in the way few things in addition to your name and family of origin ever are. Even the most materialistic among you rarely count what you have acquired in form as part of your identity. What you have acquired that is not of form, you have added to the few ideas that you hold certain. A degree earned or talent developed *is* seen as part of your identity, as part of who you are.

21.13   So too is it with beliefs. Many of you have a religious identity as well as a professional identity. Many of you have political or philosophical identities. You may call yourself Christian or doctor or democrat. You may have beliefs you hold strongly, such as a stance against capitol punishment or in favor of equal rights or environmental protection. And you may, even while recognizing, as you surely do, that these beliefs are subject to change, hold yourself to behaviors that fall within the parameters of your belief system. You think of these things as part of what make up the totality of who you are, of your personal self.

21.14   So it can be seen that there are several aspects to your personal self: an historical aspect, an aspect we will call self-image, and an aspect that has to do with beliefs.

21.15   The historical aspect is based upon your family of origin and its history as well as on the life you have led since your birth. The self-image aspect is based upon your race, ethnicity, culture, body size and shape, sex and sexual preferences and so on. The aspect that has to do with beliefs is linked to your thoughts and ideas about the world you live in and the "type" of person you feel you have chosen to be within that world. Whether you have given thought to the interconnection of these ideas you hold about yourself or not, they exist. Your world view and your view of your personal self, are inextricably bound together. In other words, the "world" you were born

187

into, regardless that it was the same "world" as all other human beings were born into, is also different than that of all other human beings. And what's more, your experiences within that world are also different than the experiences of all other human beings.

21.16   All of these things have contributed to your idea that you are a separate being and as such incapable of truly understanding or knowing your brothers and sisters, those whose personal selves and worldview cannot help but be different than your own — those whose thoughts are surely as distinct and separate as are your own.

21.17   Now however, you are being called to accept your true identity even while you retain the form of your personal self. As your true identity is that of a Self who exists in unity and the identity of your personal self is that of a self who exists in separation, this would seem impossible. Even while your belief system has changed and you believe that you exist in unity, all the things we have enumerated above will act to challenge these beliefs unless you are able to see them in a new light. No matter what you believe, while you have a body that is different from all the rest, a name that distinguishes you from some and links you with some, a nationality that separates you from other nationalities and a sex that divides you from those "opposite" you, unity will seem like a belief only.

21.18   Thus, certain things about your personal self must be accepted as aspects of your form and cease to be accepted as aspects of your identity. This will cause your existence to seem to have more of a dualistic nature for a short time while you carry observance forward into observance of your personal self. As was said at the beginning of this treatise, by the time the learning of this treatise is complete, the personal self will continue to exist *only* as the self you present to others. It will be a representation only. It will represent only the truth. The personal self will no longer be seen as your identity, but as representing your identity, an identity that has nothing to do with the thoughts of a separated mind or the circumstances of the physical body.

21.19   What might seem contradictory, is that I have said that we can also *use* the certainty you have felt about your identity for our new purpose, the purpose of the miracle that will allow you to exist as who you truly are in human form. How, you might rightly ask, can you cease to identify yourself as you always have *and* use the only identity you have been certain of for a new purpose?

21.20   The answer too will seem contradictory, for the answer lies in realizing that your former identity does not matter, even while realizing that it *will* serve your new purpose.   Further, there are even two aspects to this contradictory seeming answer.   One is that your *certainty* regarding the identity of your personal self will be useful as that certainty is translated to the thought system of the truth and aids you in becoming certain of your *true* identity.   The second is that the very differences that you seem to have will be seen as sameness by some and will attract them to you and to the truth you now will re-present.

21.21   While this has been called the time of Christ, it is obviously no longer the time of Jesus Christ.   My time came and my time ended.   The time when a single baby born of a virgin mother could change the world has passed.   The world is quite simply bigger now and the identities of your personal selves split by far more than history and far more than the oceans that separate east from west.   This is why this call to return to your Self is being sounded far and wide and why it goes out to humble and ordinary people like yourself.   There is no exclusivity to this call.   It excludes no race nor religion nor ones of either sex or sexual preference.   It but calls all to love and to live in the abundance of the truth.

21.22   In other words, it will matter not that there will be no priest or guru for those who seek the truth to turn to. It will matter not that a black man will not turn to a white man or a Muslim to a Christian. It will not matter if a young person looks to one his or her own age or turns to someone older. And yet it will matter that someone will look at you and see that you are not so different than he or she. It will matter that someone will look at you and be drawn to the truth of him- or herself that is seen reflected there. What I am saying is that your differences can serve our purpose until differences are no longer seen. What I am saying is that you can remain confident in your personal self, knowing that your personal self will serve those you are meant to serve. What you have seen as your failings or weaknesses are as valuable as are your successes and strengths. What has separated you will also unite you.

21.23   It is not being said that anyone should or will remain blind to the unity that exists beyond all barriers of seeming differences such as those of race and religion. It is simply being said that they do not matter. It will not matter if a person turns to someone "like" him- or herself to find the truth, or if a person turns to someone totally "unlike" him- or herself to find the truth. As has been said many times, willingness is the starting point and as can be surely understood, where one is willing another may not be.

21.24   There is no "other" who can follow the call meant for you. No other who can give the response you are meant to give. Do not make any false plans that give your power to others more learned of this Course than you to be the savior only you can be. Do not think that only those who are more bold than you, or who speak more eloquently, or who are better examples of a good and saintly life are those who will lead the way for others to follow. Do not give in to the idea that one special one is needed nor give to anyone a role you would not claim for yourself. No leaders and no followers are needed. This is quite obviously an old way of thinking. While no one is called to evangelize, all are called equally to represent the truth and to observance of the truth. That you all will do this in ways unique to who you are must be further addressed and seen as it relates to the relationship between the personal self and the Self, the truth and its representation and observance.

chapter 22

the True Self in Observable Form

22.1   Although the entire purpose of these treatises is to answer the question of what to do with what you have learned, chances are that this is still the primary question in your mind and heart. While you may be beginning to form ideas of what it means to live by the truth, these ideas may not seem to have much relevance or relationship to the life you currently live. While you may be happy to learn you are not called to evangelize or even to a leadership role, you know that you are called to something, and think that you as yet know not what that something is. You think that to be asked to simply "live" by the truth could not possibly be enough. You would like to know in what direction living by the truth will take you, for surely your life must change. The very precepts put forth within this course, precepts that say that the internal affects the external, seem as evidence that you will no longer be allowed the "separate" life, or private life that you have lived.

22.2   Surely there are already those called to represent not only their true Selves but this Course to the world. If this had not been the case, you would not be taking this Course. It would not be available and it would not be known to you. So even while I have said that no one is called to leadership and while I have surely meant this and do not call for leaders to amass followers, I do not mean to dissuade any of you who feel a call to represent this Course and the teachings of this Course with your lives and work. Those who feel this call are surely needed. And each of you will find the sharing of this Course to be among the easiest of ways to share what you have learned. You will almost certainly feel eagerness to share it and joy whenever and wherever you are able to do so. But some of you will find that you do no more than mention this course as the one, or one of the many teachings that have led you to the truth.

22.3   You are a beautiful representation of the truth and cannot be otherwise. You may bring this beauty to any number of walks of life, to what you currently do or to something you have always dreamt of doing. Wherever you go, whatever you do, the truth will go with you. You need no uniform nor title nor specific role for this to be the case.

22.4   Since your personal self was always meant to represent the truth of who you are, the seeds of who you are, are planted there, right within the self you have always been. There has always been within you, however, a creative tension between accepting who you are and becoming who you want to be. This tension will continue if you are unable to integrate two precepts of this course of learning into your new reality. One is the often-repeated injunction to resign as your own teacher. The other is the ability to cease all acts of comparison.

22.5   The injunction that you resign as your own teacher originated in *A Course in Miracles* and was furthered here. Along with this resignation is the concept of receiving rather than planning. Your feeling that a specific role is required of you, or that you have a specific thing to do that you need to be aware of, are functions of the pattern of the planning process that once so ruled your mind. To be willing to receive instead of plan is to break the pattern of planning.

22.6   Receiving is not an inactive state, nor one familiar to most of you. You cannot "work" at being receptive. I also do not ask you to "work" to break the pattern of planning but I do ask you to let it go and to replace it with observation.

22.7   Observation is the active state of reception, a state not confined to receiving, but a state of giving and receiving as one. Observation, as I am speaking of it and teaching it, makes you one with what you observe. Being one with what you observe causes you to know the proper response. It is in responding properly that you will know what to do.

22.8   Plans will only interfere with your response to what you are given to observe. The act of observation that you are able to do with your eyes closed is the observation of what *is*. This will relate to the future pattern of creating that we will speak of more in the next treatise.

22.9   You are impatient now to get on to the next level, the level of something new, the level that will engage you in something "to do," the level that will give an outlet for the excitement that has been building within you. You are ready to be done with the concerns of the personal self, and your attention has begun to wander from this topic even as it is being concluded.

22.10   This has been necessary so that the realization will come to you that you are ready to leave the personal self and the concerns of the personal self behind. You have needed to become bored with what has been, tired of the way things were, uninterested in matters of a personal nature.   This very readiness is what I now call your attention to as I complete this treatise with lessons concerning observation of your new Self.

22.11   The ability to cease all acts of comparison will arise out of this observation of your new Self, for you cannot observe your new Self without observing the truth that has always existed. The truth that has always existed is our oneness, and what you will observe about your new Self you will observe about all. We will be one body, one Self. No comparison will be possible.   You will realize that differences but lie in expression and representation of the truth, never in the truth itself.

22.12   I return you now to what I spoke of earlier as creative tension, the tension that exists between accepting what *is* and desiring what will be. Linking the words creative and tension is caused by the dualistic world that you have lived in, where a lag time exists between what is, and what will be. You may have, upon reading those words, thought that this creative tension would not necessarily be a good thing to give up. You do not know how to reach beyond what was for what will be without this tension. You do not yet believe in what *is*.

22.13   Observation, both of yourself and of what you desire, is an act that takes place in the here and now that *is* and brings what *is* into existence. You believe that what does not appear to exist with you in the here and now is *not*, and thus place it in a separate category, a category that only exists in the dualistic world of illusion where here and now is separate from what will be. In the new world, the world where truth reigns, there is no cause for tension for there is no world of illusion where what *is*, is separate from what will be.

22.14   Observation of what you desire, what we have referred to as "closed eyes" observation, can be likened to prayer and thus to the miracle. This is the very miracle that closes the door of duality and seals out the world where what *is* is separated from what *will be* by your effort and the time that it will take you to, through your effort, create the desired outcome. Observation of what you desire is observation of what *is*, for your desire is of God and what you desire now, contrary to what you would have desired in the early stages of this course, is the Will of God. What you desire now is the Will of God because it is your true desire, your will and God's joined as one.

22.15   Thus the creative tension can be taken from the creative act of observation without a loss of any kind.   The creative tension existed not only as a product of the duality of time, but also as a product of distrust.   It was a tension that existed between desire and accomplishment, the tension that told you that you might be able to achieve what you desire but that you also might not.   Realize that this game of chance is a pattern of the old thought system that needs to be replaced by certainty.   If you have enjoyed the game of chance, play a real game and have fun doing it.   Do not bring this attitude into your new thought system or your new life.   If you are tired of the old, be willing to be done with the old.

22.16   And so we conclude with this note of impatience with the old and the observation, the final observation, of the personal self.   You have created your personal self, and only you can look upon this personal self with the vision of creation, creating the personal self anew, seeing within it all that will serve the new, and only what will serve the new.

22.17   Observe the personal self with one last act of love and devotion, and in so doing transform the personal self into a representation of the truth.   Realize that what we have called "closed eyes" observation is really the observation of a Self beyond the personal self.   To call forth observance is to call forth the sight of your true Self.   To call forth the sight of your true Self is to call forth your true Self into observable form.   Calling the true Self forth into observable form is the end of the old and the beginning of the new.

22.18   Embrace the new as the new embraces you.   The new is but the truth that has always existed.   Go forth and live the truth with impatience only for the truth.   Hold this impatience to your Self as eagerness for the final lessons, lessons on creation of the new.

$\mathcal{A}$ Treatise on the
NEW

The Fourth Treatise

chapter 1

All Are Chosen

1.1　Let me tell you what this treatise will not be about. It will not be predictive. It will leave no one out. It will not appeal to fear nor give you cause for fear. It will not be about tools or tell you that some have the tools for accomplishment and that others do not. It will continue the view from within the embrace, an embrace and a view that is inclusive of all.

1.2　It will, however, be conclusive. It will separate truth from illusion in ways that will make some uncomfortable. It will continue to challenge your former ideas and beliefs as the previous treatises have. But it will do this only to reach a conclusion of certainty from which you can live.

1.3　In doing so, it may seem to you as if some will be left out and as if you are being told that you can achieve what many others have tried and failed to achieve. These are the types of ideas that will cause discomfort to many of you as you still find it hard to believe in your own worthiness, and particularly in your own chosenness. It is this idea of being chosen that will cause your mind to conclude that some are not chosen now and that many were not chosen in the past.

1.4　Can you choose what is unavailable for choosing? Can you choose to own another's property? Take another's husband or wife? Choosing is not taking. Choosing implies relationship. Just as there are answers to choose between on a test, some of them correct and some of them incorrect, there are some answers that are not offered to be chosen because they do not relate to the question. All of the commandments and all of the beliefs of all of the world's religions are but related to this idea of choosing, a process of the free will with which you all are endowed.

1.5 A question has been asked and a response is awaited. Are you willing to be chosen? Are you willing to be the chosen of God? All are asked. What is your answer?

1.6 Why, you might ask, is a word such as *chosen* used, when many other words would do, and when the concept of *being chosen* is one laden with so many false ideas about exclusivity? I am using this word specifically because of the historical precedent of its use. Many different groups believe they are the chosen people of God, or Buddha, or Mohammed. Many of this generation believe they are a chosen generation. Neither way of thinking is wrong. All are chosen.

1.7 An elementary example might be useful. In many countries, all are given the opportunity to go to school. This might be as easily stated as all are chosen for schooling. Some might look at this as lack of choice, saying that anything that is mandatory allows no room for choice. In their rebellion against the mandatory nature of their chosenness or opportunity, they might easily choose not to learn. The nature of life, however, is one of learning, and if they do not learn what is taught in school, they will, by default, learn what is not taught in school. If you can consider this example with no judgment, you can see it simply as a choice.

1.8 As is clearly being seen amid many school systems in the current time, the choice to not learn what is taught in school, when taken up by many, becomes a crisis in education that calls for education to change. It may signal that what is taught is no longer relevant, or that the means of teaching what is relevant no longer works. It may be a choice made regarding means or content, a choice made from fear or made from love.

But there is, in other words, no lack of choice. A choice is always made. A choice to accept or reject, say yes or say no, to learn this or to learn that, to learn now or learn later.

1.9   There but seems to be a difference in the "educated" choice and the "uneducated" choice. Many of you may look back on choices that you made and say "I would have chosen differently if I had but known" this or that. The choice is the way of coming to know. No choice is not such. No choice ever excludes anyone from coming to know his or her chosen lesson.

1.10   This curriculum is mandatory and so some have rebelled and will rebel against it. Those who do not choose to learn from the curriculum, will, like school children, learn through what is not of the curriculum because they have *chosen* another *means* of learning. *Means* is what is being spoken of here. But all means are for one end. All will learn the same content, for all are chosen, and all learning, no matter what the means, will eventually lead them to the truth of who they are.

1.11   The choice that lies before you now concerns what it is you would come to know now. The question asked throughout this course is if you are willing to make the choice to come to know your Self and God *now*. This is the same as being asked if you are willing to be the chosen of God. This is the same question that has been asked throughout the existence of time. Some have chosen to come to know themselves and God directly. Others have chosen to come to know themselves and God indirectly. These are the only choices: the choices between truth and illusion, fear and love, unity and separation, now and later. All choices will lead to knowledge of Self and God, as no choices are offered that are not such. All are chosen and so it could not be otherwise. But at the same time, it must be seen that your choice matters *in time* even if all will make the same choice eventually.

1.12   As was said within *A Treatise on the Personal Self*, even the house of illusion is held within the embrace of love, of God, of the truth. Does this sound exclusive to you? The embrace is inclusive. All are chosen.

1.13   Yet as many of you have come instinctively to feel, something is different now. You are beginning to become excited by the feeling that something different is possible: that you might just be able to achieve what others have not, that this time might just be different than any other time. Even as you begin to tentatively let this excitement grow, your loyalty to your race, species, and the past, hinders your excitement. If what you are beginning to believe might be possible is possible, and has been possible, are you to look on all of those who have come before you as failures? Has the seed of the future lain dormant in the past? Could it have been activated hundreds or thousands of years ago, by countless souls more worthy than you, and ushered in the time of heaven on earth and the end of suffering long ago? Could many have been spared who weren't? How capricious this must seem in your imaginings. What a fickle universe. What a perverse God. If an end to suffering and fear has been possible, and is possible, why has it not come to be? Why has it not been known? What could possibly make you believe it could come to be now when it didn't come to be before?

1.14   The only answer might seem to lie in the laws of evolution, the slow learning and adaptive process of man. Surely this would seem a likely answer and one to assuage your guilt and uncertainty, your fear of believing in yourself and in this time as the time to end all time. There must be something different about this time or the capabilities of those existing within it. It must be your science or technology, your advanced mental abilities, or even your leisure time that has opened up this opportunity. The only alternative would seem to be that this must simply be the chosen time and you the chosen people. If the chosen time had been two thousand years ago, life would have been different since then. If Jesus Christ was the chosen one, his life would have changed the world. If the Israelites were the chosen people, so much calamity would not have befallen them. And so the idea of choice rears its head again and wraps the simple statement that *all are chosen* in confusion.

1.15   This confusion is what this treatise will seek to dispel so that you are left with no confusion and only certainty. The only thing that will dispel this confusion and bring you the certainty that is needed to create the new world, is an understanding of creation and your role within it, both as creator and created.

1.16   As was said within *A Treatise on the Personal Self*, all notions of blame must be gone from you. You are asked to not look back with blame, for no such cause for blame exists. No cause to look back exists at all, for the truth exists in the present. This is the same as saying the truth exists within you. It is in this way that time is not real and will no longer be real to you as you come to live by the truth. It is in this way that the truth of the past still lives and that the illusion of the past never was.

1.17   The difference between this time and the time that has but seemed to have gone before has already been stated as the difference between the time of the Holy Spirit and the time of Christ. This has also been restated as the difference between the time of learning through contrast and the time of learning through observation. It is further stated here as the difference between learning by contrast and indirect communication and learning through observation and direct communication or experience. The same truth has always existed, but the choice of a means of coming to know the truth has shifted. All were chosen and all are chosen.

1.18   You have completed God's act of choosing you by choosing God. This is all the chosen people are in time —

those who have chosen God as God has chosen them. That you have chosen God *and* chosen a new means of coming to know the truth — the means of Christ-consciousness, is what has ushered in the new time.

1.19   Many came to know the truth by indirect means and shared what they came to know through similarly indirect means.   This is the nature of learning and of sharing in relationship. Means and end are one. Cause and effect are the same.   These indirect means of communicating the truth have led to your advances in science and technology, the refinement of your minds, hearts, and senses, not the reverse.   Your ancestors have done you a great service. With the means they had available   —   in   the   chosen   means   of   a   chosen consciousness united in oneness with the Holy Spirit — they passed on, indirectly, all that they came to know. This indirect means of communication is the reason for the existence of churches, and these means too have served you well.

1.20   But these indirect means of communication left much open to interpretation.   Different interpretations of indirectly received truth resulted in different religions and varying sets of beliefs that, in the way of the time, the way of learning through contrast, provided contrast through dissent.   The good in which one believed became the evil that another fought, and in the contrast learning did occur, and has continued to occur even unto this time. You have learned much of the nature of the truth by seeing what you have perceived as the contrast between good and evil.

1.21   It is the truth that you have now learned all that can be learned from this state of consciousness and that you have given your willingness to learn in a new way. The new way is here. If you are now to learn directly, you are also now to share directly. This is the way of learning in relationship. Means and end are one. Cause and effect are the same.

1.22   You have felt this shift coming and so has the world. This is the yearning we have spoken of as the proof of love's existence and of your existence in a state of unity rather than a state of separation. This yearning called you to the limits of the state of consciousness that was the time of the Holy Spirit. This limit acted upon you as a catalyst to create desire for the new. It is what has caused your growing impatience with the personal self, with acquiring all that your new learning in science and technology but seemed to offer. It is what has caused your growing desire for meaning and purpose. It is what has caused you to finally be ready to still your fear, a fear that once prevented the direct and observable learning that now is available to you.

1.23   While the state of the world and the people within it may not outwardly seem much changed from the world of your ancestors despite the advances of learning that have taken place, it is a different world. You have not known the secret yearning in the hearts of your brothers and sisters, nor have you known that it has matched your own. You may have seen the acts that this yearning has driven them to and thought, incorrectly, that the new time that is here is the end of the days of innocence. You may have thought it advantageous to have once been so clearly able to see the contrast between good and evil and feel now as if these distinctions have become more and more obscure. Some have yearned for a return to days not long past, days during which distinctions between right and wrong did seem to be more certain. But the very blurring of these edges have been the forerunners, the signs of the shift in consciousness that is occurring.

1.24   All across the world, people of the world have been demanding to learn directly, through experience, and saying "no more" to the lessons of the intermediaries. What has grown in you has grown in your children and they are not only ready, but also demanding to learn through observation and direct communication or experience. Many not yet grown to maturity have been born into the time of Christ, and do not fit within the time or the consciousness of the Holy Spirit.

1.25   For a short time, an overlap is occurring during which those unable to allow themselves to become aware of the new state of consciousness are resisting it, again indirectly. Some occupy themselves with mind and spirit numbing activities in order to block it out, having chosen to die within the state of consciousness in which they have lived. Others wish not to experience the truth directly yet, but only to experience experience. They are in the desperate throws of wanting to experience everything before they allow themselves to directly experience the truth, thinking still that the experience of the truth will exclude much that they would want to try before they give in to its pull and settle there. But all have become aware that a new experience awaits and that they stand at the threshold of choice.

1.26   Those born into the time of Christ will settle for nothing less than the truth and will soon begin looking earnestly for it. Even the ego-self will be perceived clearly by these, and they will not want it for their identity but only will accept it until another identity is offered.

1.27   Let me repeat that during the time of the Holy Spirit, some were able to come to know themselves and God through the indirect means of this state of consciousness and to pass on what they learned through indirect means. Fewer were able to achieve a state of consciousness in which direct communication was possible and come to know themselves and God directly and pass on this learning through direct means. What I am saying is that it is not impossible for those who remain unaware of the new consciousness to come to know themselves and God, and to continue to pass their learning on indirectly or through indirect communication and contrast. But this also means that the great majority will become aware of the new state of consciousness and that learning will pass through them directly through observation and direct communication or experience. It means that the last generation born into the time of the Holy Spirit will live out their lives and that soon all who remain on earth will be those born into the time of Christ.

1.28   This is the truth of the state of the world in which you exist today.

chapter 2

the True Self in Observable Form

2.1   Outward seeking is turning inward. Inward or internal discoveries are turning outward. This is a reverse, a polar reversal, that is happening worldwide and externally as well as individually and internally. It is happening. It is not predictive. I have never been and will never be predictive, for I am Christ-consciousness. Christ-consciousness is awareness of what *is*. Only an awareness of what *is*, an awareness that does not conceive of such as what was and will be, can peacefully coexist with the unity that is here and now in truth.

2.2   Again let me repeat and reemphasize my statements: where once you turned outward in your seeking and saw within what you perceived without, now you turn inward and reflect what you discover within outward. What you discover within *is* in a way that what you perceive without is not.

2.3   I have always been a proponent of The Way of Christ-consciousness as The Way to Self and God.

2.4   There was no Way or path or process back to God and Self before me. It was the time of man wandering in the wilderness. I came as a representation or demonstration of The Way. This is why I have been called "The way, the truth and the life." I came to show The Way to Christ-consciousness, which is The Way to God and Self. But I also came to provide an intermediary, for this is what was desired: a bridge between the human or forgotten self, and the divine or remembered Self. Jesus the man was the intermediary who ushered in the time of the Holy Spirit by calling the Holy Spirit to possess the human or forgotten self with the spirit of the divine or remembered Self. Although God never abandoned the humans who seeded the Earth, the humans, in the state of the forgotten self, could not know God because of their fear. I revealed a God of Love and the Holy Spirit provided for indirect and less fearful means of communion or communication with God.

2.5   The people of the Earth and all that were created have always been the beloved of God because Love is the means of creation. The people of the Earth, and all that were created, were created through union and relationship. Creation through union and relationship is still The Way and The Way has come into the time of its fullness.

2.6   The production that so has so long occupied you will now serve you as you turn your productive and reproductive instincts to the production and reproduction of relationship and union.

2.7   But before we can proceed forward, I must return to and dispel any illusion you may have of superiority over those who came before. That those who came before did not become aware of their true nature does not mean that it did not exist. That there are others living among you in this time who will not become aware of their true nature does not mean that it does not exist within them. You are no *more* accomplished than anyone has been, or is, or will be. The truth of who you are is *as* accomplished as the truth of all of your brothers and sisters from the beginning of time until the end of time. Any text that tells you that you or those of your kind or time are more or better than any other is not speaking the truth. This is why we began with the chosen and will return again and again to the statement that *all are chosen.*

2.8   I belabor this point because you literally cannot proceed to full awareness while ideas such as *more* and *better* remain in you. This is not about evolution unless you wish to speak of

209

evolution in terms of awareness. You must realize that if you were to see into the eyes and hearts of any human from any time with true vision, you would see the accomplished Self there. There can be no judgment carried forward with you and when you continue to believe in a process of evolution that has made you better than those who came before, you are carrying judgment. While you continue to believe that being chosen means that some are not chosen, you are carrying judgment. While you continue to believe that a final judgment will separate the good from the evil, you are carrying judgment.

2.9   I also belabor this point because those of you familiar with the Bible, upon hearing words such as the end of time or the fullness of time, think of the predictions of the Biblical end of time. I speak of this because it is in your awareness and because many false interpretations of this time as a time of judgment and of separating the chosen people from all others abound. All are chosen. All are chosen with love and without judgment.

2.10   The idea of separation is an idea that is not consistent with the idea of unity. If you proceed into this new time thinking that this new time will separate you from others, or cause you, as *the chosen*, to be separate, you will not become fully aware of the new time. Full awareness of the new is what this treatise seeks to accomplish and so it is necessary to belabor these false ideas that would keep you from this awareness. If you think you can observe in judgment you do not understand the definition of observation provided in *A Treatise on the Personal Self*.

2.11   Being first does not mean being better. That I was the first to demonstrate what you can be does not mean I am better than you. Just as in your sporting events, a "first" is applauded, and soon a new record replaces that record-setting first, just as someone had to be "first" to fly a plane or land on the moon, being first implies only that there will be a second and a third.

That attention and respect is given to those who first achieve anything of any merit is but a way of calling all others to know what they can achieve. One may desire to best a sporting record and another to follow the first man into space and the one who desires to best a sporting record may feel no desire to follow the first man into space and vice versa, and yet, what one achieves but opens the door for others and this is known to you. Even those who did not desire to fly in a plane when this feat was first accomplished have since flown in planes.

2.12   Similarly, those who have achieved "first place" do so realizing that the elevated "place" they briefly hold is of a finite nature and that others will soon do the same and that those who follow in time will do so more easily, with less effort, and with even greater success. They may consider themselves "better than" for a moment in time, but those who do will be bitterly disappointed as their moment passes. Despite the necessity for a confidence that has led them to achieve their desired end, most who so achieve and become the first to set records, discover, or invent the new, are not aware of themselves as "better than" for their goal was not to be better than anyone but themselves. Surely many desire to be "the best" as a means to glorify the ego, but few of these succeed for the ego cannot be glorified.

2.13   Thus, you must examine your intention even now and remove from it all ideas that were of the old way. You would not be here if you were still interested in glorifying the ego. You also are not yet completely certain of your Self, and in your uncertainty, still subject to the patterns of thought of the old. Many of these patterns do not concern me for they will fall away of themselves as your awareness of the new grows. But these few on which I linger will prevent your awareness of the new from growing and so must be consciously left behind.

2.14   It is difficult for you, because of the patterns of the past, to believe that you are chosen to be the pioneers into a new time without believing that you are special. This is one of the many reasons we have worked to dispel your ideas of specialness. One of the best means for us to clarify the lack of specialness implied in the statement that all are chosen, is through your observation of yourself.

2.15 The ability to observe what the Self expresses was among the original reasons for this chosen experience. Observe now the expressions of the self you are and have been. Although you are different now than you were as a child, and different now than you were a few years ago, and different now than when you began your learning of this course, you are not other than who you have always been. Who you are now was there when you were a child, and there in all the years since then, and there before you began your learning of this course. Your *awareness* of the Self that you are now was not present in the past, but you can truly now, with the devotion of the observant, see that the Self you are now was indeed present, and was the truth of who you were then as now.

2.16 How, then, could you possibly observe any others without knowing that the truth of who they are is present even though it might seem not to be? This is the power of the devotion of the observant that you are called to, the power of cause and its effect. This is the power you now have within you, the power to observe truth rather than illusion. This is the power to observe what *is*. This is Christ-consciousness.

2.17 I repeat, this is the power to observe what *is*. It is not about observing a potential for what could be if your brother or sister would just follow in the way that has been shown to you. It is about observing what *is*. The power to observe what *is* is what will keep you unified with your brothers and sisters rather than separating you from them. There is no power without this unity. You cannot see "others" as other than who they are and know your power. You must see as I see and see that all are chosen.

212

2.18 Only from this shared vision, this observation of what *is* can you begin to produce unity and relationship *through* unity and relationship.

2.19 This is why it has long been stated that you are not called to evangelize or convince anyone of the merits of this course of study. This is just a course of study. Those whom you would seek to evangelize or convince are as holy as your Self. This holiness need only be observed. When you think in terms of evangelizing or convincing, you think in terms of future outcome rather than in terms of what already is. This type of thinking will not serve the new or allow you full awareness of the new.

2.20 Can you remember this, blessed sons and daughters of the most high? Your brothers and sisters are as holy as your Self. Holiness is the natural harmony of all that was created as it was created.

2.21 Now I tell you something else and hope you will remember it and bid it true. Each day is a creation and holy too. Not one day is meant to be lived in a struggle with what it brings. The power to observe what *is* relates to everything that exists with you, including the days that make up your life in time and space. Observing what *is* unites you with the present in that it unites you with what *is* rather than with what you perceive to be.

2.22 Observation of what *is* is a natural effect of the cause of a heart and mind joined in unity. This first joining in unity, the joining of heart and mind, joins the physical and the spiritual world in a relationship of which you can be more and more steadily aware. It is a new relationship. Unity always existed. Oneness always existed. God always existed. But you separated yourself from direct awareness of your *relationship* with unity, with oneness and with God, just as you separated yourself from relationship with the wholeness of the pattern of creation. You have believed in God and perhaps in some concept of unity or oneness, but you have also denied even the possibility of experiencing your own direct relationship with God, or the possibility that your life is a direct experience of the pattern of unity or oneness that is creation.

2.23   Think of this denial now, for it is still evident in the pattern of your thinking. We have spoken of this within the text of *A Course of Love* as your inability to realize the relationship that exists with the unseen and even the seen. You have moved through life believing you have relationships with family and friends and coworkers, occasionally acknowledging brief relationships that develop with acquaintances or strangers, connections that feel real with like-minded associates for brief periods of time, but still essentially seeing yourself moving through life alone with few sustaining connections save for special relationships, and with little purpose implied in the brief encounters you have with others.   You have watched the news and developments in parts of the world far away from you and at times are aware of ecological and sociological connections, or of other occurrences that are likely to have an impact on your life or on your part of the world. But unless you believe in the ability of what happens to have an effect on you, you do not consider yourself to have a relationship with the occurrence.

2.24   With your new understanding of observance must come a new understanding of relationship and the ability of the devotion of the observant to affect relationship.

2.25   Yet we have strayed here from the overriding idea of what I have revealed to you. A *new* relationship now exists between the physical and spiritual.   It is not an indirect relationship but a direct relationship.   It exists and you are becoming aware of its existence.   You will increasingly be unable to deny it and you will not want to.   As you allow awareness of this relationship to grow in you, you will learn the lessons that are being spoken of within this treatise.

2.26   This new relationship is the only state in which observation of what *is* can occur. The separated state was nothing more than the disjoining of heart and mind, a state in which mind attempted to know without the relationship of the heart and so merely perceived its own creations rather than the creations birthed in unity.

2.27   Let this idea gestate a moment within you and reveal to you the truth of which it speaks. The separated state of the mind created its own separate world. Cause and effect are one. The perceived state of separation created the perceived state of a separate world. The real state of union, returned to you through the joining of mind and heart, will now reveal to you the truth of what was created and allow you to create anew.

2.28   This state of union is what differentiated me from my brothers and sisters at the time of my life on earth. Because my state of consciousness, a state of consciousness we are calling Christ-consciousness, allowed me to exist in union and relationship with all, I could see my brothers and sisters "in Christ" or in their true nature. I saw them in union and relationship, where they saw themselves in separation. This ability to see in union and relationship is the *shared* vision to which you are called.

2.29   You have lived with the vision of the separated self for so long that you cannot imagine what *shared* vision will mean, and do not recognize it when you experience it. This is why you can still think of observance of what *is* as a game of make believe and feel that you will have to trick yourself into believing that you see love where there is cause for fear. You must remember that you are now called to see without judgment. To see without judgment is to see truly. You need

215

not look for good or bad, but only need be steadily aware that you can only see in one of two ways — with love or fear.

2.30   You expect yourself to still see with the eyes of separation rather than with the shared vision of which I speak. You expect to see bodies and events moving through your days as you have in the past. And yet your vision has already changed, although you are not aware of the extent of this change. Realize now that you have come to recognize unity. You no longer see each person and event as separate, with no relation to the whole. You *are* beginning to see the connections that exist and this is the beginning.

2.31   Examine what you may have felt the onset of true vision would mean. Have you considered this question? Have you expected to see in the same way but more lovingly? Have you thought you might begin to recognize those who, like you, are joined with me in Christ-consciousness? Have you suspected that you might see in ways literally different? That you might see auras or halos, signs and clues previously unseen? Have you included other senses in your idea of "sight"? Have you thought your instincts will be sharpened and that you will know with an inner knowing that will aid the sight of your eyes?

2.32   All of these things are possible. But true vision is seeing relationship and union. It is the opposite of seeing with the eyes and the attitude of separation. It is seeing with an expectation first and foremost of revelation. It is believing that you exist in relationship and union with all and that each encounter is one of union and relationship and *purpose*...purpose that will be revealed to you because you exist in union with the Source and Cause of revelation.

2.33   Seeing with the vision of Christ-consciousness is already upon you. You are in the process of learning what it means. This treatise is here to help you do so. Learning to see anew is the precursor of learning to create anew. Creating anew is the precursor of the coming of the new world. Remember, only from a shared vision of what *is* can you begin to produce unity and relationship *through* unity and relationship. This is your purpose now, and this the curriculum to guide you to the fulfillment of your purpose.

chapter 3

Natural Vision

3.1   Observation is an extension of the embrace that in turn makes the embrace observable. The embrace is not an action so much as a state of being. Awareness of the embrace comes from the vision of which I have just begun to speak.

3.2   Observation and vision are closely linked but not the same. Observation has to do with the elevation of the personal self. Vision has to do with what cannot be elevated. Vision has to do with the divine pattern, the unity that binds all living things. Observation is the means of seeing this binding pattern in physical form.

3.3   The personal self is still in need of being elevated — elevated to its original nature — by its original nature or intent. The devotion of the observant will return you to your original purpose. The vision of Christ-consciousness will take you beyond it.

3.4   Original intent has everything to do with the nature of things for original intent is synonymous with cause. The original intent of this chosen experience was the expression of the Self of love in observable form. This original intent or cause formed the true nature of the personal self capable of being observed in relationship. The displacement of the original intent, while it did not change the original cause, formed a false nature for the personal self. This displacement of the original intent can be simply stated as the displacement of love with fear. It is as simple as that. Yet the *way* in which each of you have interpreted this displacement has come to seem quite complex.

3.5   You may not feel that you have ever intended to live in fear. But the displacement of the original intent was so complete that each life began with fear and proceeded from this beginning continually reacting to fear. While the original intent remained within you and caused you to attempt to express a Self of love despite your fear, fear has thwarted your every effort and caused the very effort that has continued the cycle of fear. To have to *try* to be who you are and to express who you are is the result of the displacement of the nature of love with the nature of fear. What we now are about is reversing this displacement and returning you to your true nature.

3.6   For every being there is a *natural state* that is joyful, effortless, and full of love. For every being existing in time there is also an unnatural state of being. Both states of being — the natural and the unnatural — exist in relationship. While relationship is what has kept you forever unable to be separate and alone, relationship is also what has kept you forever unable to return to your natural state of being. The fear that was birthed along with the erroneously inherited idea that it was your nature to be separate and alone, made relationships fearful as well. Trust became something to be earned. Even the most loving parent, like unto your most loving image of God, having brought a child into a fearful world, became subject to the tests of time. Thus did the world become a world of effort with all things in it and beyond it, including God, weighed and balanced against the idea of fear.

3.7   Now, as we reverse this set of circumstances, and replace the world of fear with a world of love, there can be no more weighing of love against fear. God did not create fear and will not be judged by it. All judgment is the cause of fear and this effort to weigh love's strength against fear's veracity. While you chose to believe and live in a world the nature of which was fear, you could not know God. You could not know God because you judged God from within the nature of fear, believing fear to be your natural state.

3.8   As the natural state of love is returned to you, judgment falls away because vision will arise. With the onset of the vision of love, many of you will make one final judgment in which you find everything to be good and full of love. Once all has been judged with the vision of love, judgment is over naturally for it has served its purpose. This is the final judgment.

3.9   The vision that will arise in you now is not new. It is your natural vision, the vision of love. What is new is the elevation of the personal self that will be caused by the return of your natural state of love. This is where observation comes in.

3.10   Vision will allow you to see the nature of the world and all that exists within it truly. Observation will allow you to elevate the personal self to its rightful place within the nature of a world of love.

3.11   Vision is the natural *means* of knowing of all who were created in love. Observation is the natural *means* of sharing what is known in physical form.

3.12   The physical form is not the natural or original form of the created. Vision is the *means* by which the original nature of the created can once again be known. Observation is the *means* by which the original nature of the created can newly be seen in physical form. Once the original nature of the created becomes observable in physical form, physical form will surpass what it once was and become the *new* nature of the created. There is no reason why the original nature of your being cannot become a being the nature of which is form if you so choose it to be. There *is* a reason why the original nature of your being cannot exist in a form unnatural to love. A form whose nature is fear cannot house the creation of love.

3.13   Man has striven since the beginning of time to be done with the separated state of a being of form, and at the same time to hang on to life, not realizing that what exists in form does not have to be separate and alone; not realizing that what lives does not have to die. That the nature of form can change. That the nature of matter is one of change. That the nature, even of form, once returned to its natural state of love, is one of unity and everlasting life.

3.14   The idea of everlasting life in form has seemed a curse to some, a miracle to others. Death comes as destruction to some, as new life to others. Either way is but your choice. Your attachment to life has kept you alive in form. Your attachment to death has kept your form subject to the cycle of decay and rebirth. There is another alternative.

3.15   The promise of life everlasting was not an empty promise. It is a promise that has been fulfilled. It is you who have chosen the means. Now a new choice is before you.

chapter 4

the Inheritance of Everlasting Life

4.1   Everywhere within your world you see the pattern of life-everlasting. Where there is a pattern of life-everlasting, there is everlasting life. Means and end are one, cause and effect the same.

4.2   The pattern of life-everlasting is one of changing form. It is one that is revealed on Earth by birth and death, decay and renewal, seasons of growth and seasons of decline. This is the pattern of creation taken to extremes. Inherent within the extreme is the balance. Even in the biblical description of creation was a day of rest spoken of. Creation balanced with rest is the pattern that has been taken to extremes within your world. You think of birth as creation and death as rest. You do not realize that your nature, and the nature of your life, like that of all around you, is governed by seasons natural to the state of love, seasons of regeneration.

4.3   In your history, generations pass, through death, to allow for new generations to be born. As your planet has reached a state of growth known as over-population, this balance between old generations and new seems necessary and even crucial. One generation *must* pass to make room for the new.

4.4   Even before the planet reached the state of over-population, this idea was much in evidence. The passing of a parent was seen, particularly historically, as the time of the child of the parent coming into his or her inheritance or time of fullness. The *power* and prestige, the earthly wealth of the parent, passed historically to the son.

4.5   This is one of the reasons that I came in the form of the "Son of God." In the time in which I lived, the idea of inheritance was an even stronger idea, an idea with much more power than in current times. Inherent within the idea of inheritance was an idea of passing as well as an idea of continuity. What belonged to the father passed to the son and thereafter belonged to the son. What was of the father continued with the son.

4.6   What my life demonstrated was a capacity for inheritance not based upon death. My life, death, and resurrection revealed the power of inheritance, the power of the Father, as one of life-giving union. I called you then, and I call you now, to this inheritance.

4.7   This idea of inheritance is a natural idea arising from the nature of creation itself. It is an idea of continuity that is an idea consistent with that of creation. There is no discontinuity within creation. Like begets like. Life begets life. Thus is revealed the pattern of life-everlasting.

4.8   Changing form is part of the pattern of life-everlasting. The change in the form you now occupy, the change I have spoken of as that of elevation of the personal self, is a natural part of the pattern of life-everlasting. It is long over-due. It is long over-due because you have rejected rather than accepted your inheritance.

4.9   This is why this treatise is called *A Treatise on the New.* There has not been a time on Earth in which the inheritance of God the Father was accepted, save by me. This is why this time is spoken of as the time of fullness. It is the time during which you have within your awareness the ability to come into your time of fullness by accepting the inheritance of your

Father. You have the awareness and thus the ability to accept the continuity of life-everlasting.

4.10   Lest this sound like the ranting of your science fiction, and cause you to turn deaf ears to the knowledge I would impart, let me assure you that immortality is not the change of which I speak. You are not mortal, and so a word that speaks of an opposite to what you are not and have never been is not the accurate word. I do not speak of bodies living forever instead of living for what you call a lifetime — be it a lifetime of twenty, or fifty, or ninety years. Life has continuously been prolonged without a substantial change in the nature of life. To think of living on and on as you have lived your life thus far would not appeal to many of you. Those aged and contemplating death might wish for prolonged life, but many of these same welcome death as the end to suffering and strife. To continue on endlessly with life as it has been would only relegate more and more to lives not worth living.

4.11   What is it then, of which I speak? If you still must look ahead and see death looming on the horizon, how can it be that I speak of life-everlasting? Am I but using new words to repeat what you have heard in various form from various religions and systems of belief for countless ages? Am I but calling you to a happy death and an after-life in heaven?

4.12   I am calling you to the new. I am calling you to transform. I am calling you to Christ-consciousness. I am calling you to everlasting consciousness even while you still abide in form. To be cognizant or aware of everlasting consciousness while you still abide in form is to be fully aware that you have life-everlasting.

4.13   Being fully aware that you have life-everlasting is totally different than having faith in an after-life. Faith is based upon the unknown. If the unknown were not unknown faith would not be necessary. Faith *will* become unnecessary, as life-everlasting becomes *known* to you.

4.14 This knowing will come from the return of true vision. True vision sees life-everlasting where perception but saw finite life and mortal bodies. Once vision and Christ-consciousness have returned to you, the *means* of life-everlasting will be understood as a choice. Because there was no relationship save that of intermediaries between the human and the divine, there was no choice but to end the separated state in order to return to unity through death. Once the return to unity has occurred in form, the decision to continue in form or to not continue in form will be yours.

4.15 Continuity is an attribute of relationship, not of matter. It is only in the relationship of matter to the divine that matter can become divine and thus eternal. If you can abide in unity while in human form, you will have no cause, save your own choice, to leave human form. To abide in unity is to abide in your natural state, a state of life-everlasting. To abide in a state of separation is to abide in an unnatural state from which you eventually will seek release.

4.16 Although this discussion is likely to cause many of you serious doubts about the truth and applicability of this course, this discussion is necessary to your awareness of Christ-consciousness. To believe that you are mortal is to believe that you must die to the personal self of form in order to be reborn as a true Self. This is an old way of thinking. Have we not worked throughout this Course to return your true identity to you *now*? The joining of heart and mind in relationship is the joining of the personal self with the true Self *in the reality in which you exist now.* Remember, the heart must abide in the reality where you think you are. Only through your mind's acceptance of your new reality has the heart been freed to exist in the new reality that is the state of unity and relationship.

4.17   Can you not see the necessity of removing the idea that your true Self will be returned to you only through death? What purpose would this Course serve if it were just another preview of what to expect after you die? What difference would this make to your way of living or to the world in which you live?

4.18   What purpose will death serve when your true Self has joined with your physical form? You will see it simply as the transformation it has always been, the transformation from singular consciousness to Christ-consciousness. Form has been but a representation of singular consciousness. As form becomes a representation of Christ-consciousness it will take on the nature of Christ-consciousness of which my life was the example life. To sustain Christ-consciousness in form is creation of the new. My one example life could not sustain Christ-consciousness for those who came after me but could only be an example. What you are called to do is to, through your multitude, sustain Christ-consciousness, and create the union of the human and the divine as a new state of being. This union will take you beyond the goal of expressing your Self in form because this goal but reflected the desire for a temporary experience. The temporary experience has been elongated because of the appeal of the physical experience. What this treatise is saying to you is that *if* the physical experience appeals to you, and *if* you create the union of the human and the divine as a new state of being, this choice will be eternally yours. It will be a choice of your creation, a creation devoid of fear. It will be a new choice.

chapter 5

the Energy of Creation and the Body of Christ

5.1   Life-everlasting in form is not your only choice. As many of you believed that I was the Son of God and more than a man before my birth, during my lifetime, and after my death and resurrection, so are you. So are all who came before me and all who came after me. All that being a Son of God means is that you represent the continuity of creation and that your fulfillment lies in the acceptance of your true inheritance.

5.2   This could as easily be stated as your being a Song of God. You are God's harmony, God's expression, God's melody. You, and all that exist with you, form the orchestra and chorus of creation. You might think of your time here as that of being apprentice musicians. You must *learn* or *relearn* what you have forgotten so that you can once again join the chorus. So that you can once again be in harmony with creation. So that you can express yourself within the relationship of unity that is the whole of the choir and the orchestra. So that you can realize your accomplishment in union and relationship. So that you can join your accomplishment with that of all others and become the Body of Christ.

5.3   The many forms are made one body through Christ-consciousness. The one body is one energy given many expressions in form. The same life-force courses through all that exists in matter in the form of this energy. Awareness of this one Source of energy, and that this one energy exists in everything and creates the life in everything, is Christ-consciousness. It is also what we have been referring to as heart and as the center of your being. What would the center of your being be but the Source of your being?

5.4   In order for your body to live, this one Energy had to enter your form and exist where you think you are. This is the Energy of Love, the Energy of Creation, the Source that is known as God. Since you are clearly alive, this Energy exists within you as it exists in all else that lives. It is one Energy endlessly able to materialize in an inexhaustible variety of forms. It is one Energy endlessly able to dematerialize and rematerialize in an inexhaustible variety of form. But form does not contain It and is not required for Its existence or expression. How could form contain God? How could form contain the Energy of Creation?

5.5   Your form does not contain your heart, or the Energy of Creation, or God. Your form is but an extension of this Energy, a representation of it. You might think of this as a small spark of the Energy that has created a living universe existing within you and uniting you to all that has been created. You are the substance of the universe. The same Energy exists in the stars of the heavens and the waters of the ocean that exists in you. This Energy is the form and content of the embrace. It is within you, and It surrounds you, and It encompasses you. It is you and all who exist with you. It is the Body of Christ. It is like unto what the water of the ocean is to the living matter that exists within it. The living matter that exists within the ocean has no need to search for God. It lives in God. So do you.

5.6   God can thus be seen as the All of Everything, and life, or the Body of Christ, as all that makes up the seemingly individual parts of the All of Everything. Christ-consciousness is your awareness of this.

5.7   Just as your finger is but one part of your body, without being separate from your body or other than your body, you are

228

part of the Body of Christ, the Body of Energy that makes up the universe.

5.8   Your finger is governed by the larger body, intricately connected to signals of the brain, to the linking muscles and bones, to the blood that flows and the heart that beats. Your finger does not act independently of the whole. You might say that your finger does not, then, have free will.   It cannot express itself independently of the whole.

5.9   The same is true of you! You cannot express yourself independently of the whole! It is as impossible as it would be for the finger to do so. And yet you think that this is possible and that this is the meaning of free will. Free will does not make the impossible possible. Free will makes the possible probable. It is *probable* that you will use your free will in order to be who you are. But it is not guaranteed! It is your choice and your choice alone that is the only guarantee. This is the meaning of free will.

5.10   To align your will with the Will of God is to make the choice for Christ-consciousness, to make the choice to be aware of who you truly are. It is to know your Self as my brother or sister *in Christ*; to be the Body of Christ.

5.11   I am calling you to make this choice now. This is not a choice automatic to you in human form or even upon the death of your human form. When you die, you do not die to who you are or to who you think you are. You do not die to choice. At the time of death you are assisted in ways not formerly possible to you in form, to make the choice to be who you are. You are shown in ways that the body's eyes were unable to see, the glory of your true nature. You are given the chance, just as you are being given the chance now, to choose your true nature with your free will.

5.12   Because you have now made a new choice, a collective choice as one body, one consciousness, to end the time of the intermediary and to begin to learn directly, you are given the same opportunity now that was formerly reserved for you only after your death. It was formerly only after your death that you chose direct revelation by God. Think about this now and you will see that it is true. You hoped to live a good life and at the end of that life to know God. Your vision of the after-life was one in which God revealed Himself to you and in that revelation transformed you. The direct revelations that will come to you now will transform you as surely as did those that came to so many others after death.

5.13   If you have believed in any kind of after-life at all, you have perhaps thought of the after-life as having two sides. Some have thought of this as heaven and hell; others as all or nothing. Many of you have thought of it as a time of judgment. But I tell you truly: It is no different than the time that is upon you right now.   The after-life has simply been a time of increased choice because it has been a time of increased awareness. Loosed of the body and the body's limited vision, real choice has been revealed to those having experienced death.   At that time it is your judgment of your *self* and your ability to believe in the glory that is yours, that determines the way in which your life will continue. The same is true right now!   For this is the time of Christ and thus of your ability to choose Christ-consciousness, the consciousness returned to those loosed of the body by death. Being loosed of the body by death was the chosen means of the time of the intermediary, the chosen means of attaining Christ-consciousness and direct revelation. The elevation of the personal self in this time of Christ can be the new choice.

chapter 6

A New Choice

6.1 Now I ask you to consider the part you play in the creation of this all-encompassing consciousness. Your state of consciousness, be you alive or dead, asleep or awake, literally or figuratively, is a *part* of the consciousness that is Christ-consciousness. This is why you hear differing reports of the after-life from those who have experienced temporary death. It is why you hear differing words and scenarios attributed to me and other life-giving spirits, both historically and currently. What you envision, imagine, desire, hold as being possible, *is* possible, because you make it so. It is your interaction, both individually and collectively with the consciousness that is *us*, that creates probable futures rather than guaranteed futures.

6.2 The only guarantee I can offer you is the guarantee that you are who I say you are and that I speak the truth concerning your identity and inheritance. What you choose to do with this knowledge is still up to you. What you choose to create with this knowledge is still up to you.

6.3 Thus, those who believe that only some will be chosen *can* create a scenario in which it appears that some are chosen and some are not. Those who believe that life-everlasting includes life on other worlds can create a scenario in which it appears that some live on one world and some on another. But I say to you that any scenario that separates my brothers and sisters from one another and the one life-giving energy that unites us all will but continue life as it has been but in different form. The realization of unity is the binding realization that will return all, as one body, to the natural state of Christ-consciousness.

6.4   In this time of Christ, this time of direct revelation and direct sharing, the probable future you imagine, envision, desire, will be what you create. This is the power of the devotion of the observant. A *shared* vision of unity and a return of *all* to the state natural to all, is what I ask you to imagine, envision, and desire.

6.5   I ask you to share a vision of what *is*, the very vision of what *is* that *is* Christ-consciousness. It is a vision of the perfection of creation. It is a vision of unity and relationship in harmony. It excludes no one and no one's choice and no one's vision. Your brothers and sisters who do not choose their natural state still are who they are and as holy as yourself. Your brothers and sisters who choose alternative visions are still who they are and as holy as yourself. All choices are forever encompassed by the embrace. There is no wrong choice. No one is excluded. All are chosen.

6.6   There is room in the universe, dear brothers and sisters, for everyone's choice. I call you to a new choice, but not to intolerance of those who are not ready to make it. I call you to a new choice with the full realization that your choice alone will affect millions of your brothers and sisters — as long as — and this is crucial, you do not give in to ideas of separation and disunity.

6.7   Christ-consciousness is not a static state of beliefs anymore than singular consciousness is. Christ-consciousness is consciousness of what *is*. While consciousness of what *is* leaves not the room for error that perception leaves, it leaves open room for creation. In each moment, what *is*, while still existing in the one truth of God's laws of love, can find many expressions. You can exist in Christ-consciousness, as have many others of the past, and through your existence in Christ-consciousness, affect much with what you envision, imagine, and desire, in love, without changing the world and the nature of the human being any more than have those who have come before. The changes those who have existed in Christ-consciousness have wrought have been great, but they did not sustain Christ-consciousness, primarily because they were unable to share Christ-consciousness directly because of individual and collective choice.

6.8   You have the unequalled opportunity now, because you exist in the time of Christ, to directly share Christ-consciousness and to sustain Christ-consciousness. You can pass on the inheritance you accept in this fullness of time. In this time of unity, dedicate all thought to unity. Accept no separation. Accept all choices. Thus are all chosen in the fullness of time.

chapter 7

An End to Learning

7.1   Christ-consciousness will be temporary or sustainable depending on your ability to refrain from judgment. What *is* flows from Love and knows not judgment. All that you envision, imagine, and desire with love *must* be without judgment or it will be false envisioning, false imagining, false desire. This simply means *false*, or not consistent with the truth. It does not mean wrong or bad and is itself no cause for judgment. It is simply an alternative that will draw you out of Christ-consciousness and not allow it to be sustainable.

7.2   That you are living in the time of Christ does not mean that you will automatically realize Christ-consciousness, just as living in the time of the Holy Spirit did not mean that you would automatically realize the consciousness of the spirit that was your intermediary. But just as during the time of the Holy Spirit, your understanding of your Self and God grew through the indirect means that were available to you, during the time of Christ, your understanding of your Self and God cannot help but grow through the direct and observable means now available. Just as in the time of the Holy Spirit the spirit was available to all as intermediary, during the time of Christ, Christ-consciousness is available to all.

7.3   Those of you who have acquired Christ-consciousness and are now learning the vision of Christ-consciousness must realize the many choices that will seem to lie before you and your brothers and sisters in this time. The understanding of the unity that creates and sustains all living things will now be as close to the surface of consciousness as was, during the time of the Holy Spirit, the understanding that man is imbued with spirit. People, both religious and non-religious, those who consider themselves spiritual and those who consider themselves pragmatists, will hold this understanding within their grasp. Many will be surprised by experiences of unity and know not what to make of them. Those who attempt to figure them out will come ever closer to the truth by means of science, technology, and even art and literature. Those who allow themselves to experience revelation will enter Christ-consciousness.

7.4   Those who sustain Christ-consciousness will abide within it free of judgment. They will not seek to create their version of a perfect world and to force it upon others, but will abide within the perfect world that *is* in the vision of Christ-consciousness. This perfect world will be observable to them and in them. It will be revealed to them and through them. It will be revealed to them through what they can envision, imagine, and desire without judgment. It will not take the effort of their bodies, but the freedom of a consciousness joined in unity, a consciousness able to envision, imagine, and desire without judgment and without fear.

7.5   This is why all fear, including the fear of death, needs to be removed from you despite the radical sounding nature of life-everlasting. You cannot sustain Christ-consciousness while fear remains in you, just as you cannot sustain Christ-consciousness while judgment remains in you. Why? Because it is not in the nature of Christ; it is not in the nature of the Christ-Self to know fear or judgment. What we are speaking of is abiding in your natural state. Your natural state is one free of fear and judgment. This is all that makes the difference between your natural state and your unnatural state. As your natural state returns to you through a heart and mind joined in unity, your body too will exist or abide within this natural state. It cannot help to, as it, just like your heart, exists in the state or reality in which you think you are. The only thing that has created an unreal reality for your heart and body has been the inability of the mind to join the truth with your conscious awareness. While your mind did not accept the truth of your identity or the reality of love without fear, it existed in a reality of fear and judgment, and bound heart and body to this reality. Your heart has now heard the appeal of this course and worked with your mind to bring about this acceptance of the truth, a truth your heart has always known but has been unable to free you to accept without the mind's cooperation.

7.6   The mind, once released from the ego's thought system, has but to relearn the thought system of the truth. Your mind, heart, and body have joined in alignment to bring this learning about. They now exist in harmony. Your mind and heart in union have brought harmony to your body. Sustaining this harmony will keep your body in perfect health, even while the manner of this perfection of your health will remain one of many options.

7.7   You will realize that what *is* is optimal to your learning. But you will also realize that an end to your learning is in sight. Once Christ-consciousness, and the ability to know what *is* has reached a state of sustainability in you, your need for learning and the conditions of learning ends. Being in harmony with poor health, and learning the lesson that it has come to impart to you, will return you to good health. Your poor health is, in other words, no cause for judgment, as it is the perfect health, now, in the past, and in the future, to bring you the lessons you would learn in order to return you to your Self and the unity of Christ-consciousness. The same is true of all conditions of all learning everywhere. The conditions are perfect for optimal learning. This is the nature of the universe. These conditions are perfect not only for individual learning, but for shared learning, learning in community, and learning as a species.

7.8   But let me again emphasize that the conditions of learning will no longer be needed once learning has occurred.

236

The student no longer needs to attend school once the desired curriculum is learned, *except* through their own choice. Again let me remind you that no choice is wrong. Some will choose to continue to learn through the full variety of the human experience even after it is unnecessary. Why? Because it is a choice, pure and simple. But because it is an educated choice, an enlightened choice, a free choice due to the learning that has already occurred, the choice will be one guided by love and thus be a joyous choice and ensure a joyous life. These choices will *change* the world.

7.9   But the choice many of you will make — the choice to move from learning to creating — will *create a new world.*

chapter 8

To Come To Know

8.1　You are now beginning to reach the stage of understanding where in you can realize that it was not some separate "you" or some entity without form who, at some point in time, chose to express love in physical form, and so began this experience of human life.　You are now beginning to be able to understand that it was God who made this choice.　That this was the Creator making a choice and creation's response was the universe, which is an expression of God's love, an expression of God's choice, a representation of God's intent.

8.2　I say you are only now beginning to reach a stage where you can understand this, but what I really mean is that you are only now reaching a stage where in you can know, within your inner being, that this is the truth.　I say this because it is only now that you can come to know this truth without reverting to old ideas of not having had "yourself" any choice in the matter, or reverting to old ideas of blaming God for all that has ensued since this choice.　I say this because only now are you beginning to be ready to hear that you and God are the same.　That when I say "God made a choice" I am not saying that you did not.　I am saying that a choice was made within the one mind, the one heart and that this was your choice as well as God's choice.　It was one choice made in unity.　It was the choice of all for life-everlasting and life-ever expressing.　It was the choice for creation, for creation is the expression of love.

8.3　The heart of God is the "center" of the universe, as your own heart is the center of your being.　The mind of God is the Source of all ideas, just as "your" mind is the source of your ideas.

8.4   Let us dwell again, for just a moment before we let this dwelling in the past go forever, on what has "gone wrong" with God's expression of love.

8.5   Creation in form had a starting point. This is the nature of everything that lives in form. It has a starting point from which it grows into its time of fullness. Creation on the scale at which God creates produced the universe, or in actuality, many universes. These universes grew and changed, ebbed and flowed, materialized and dematerialized in natural cycles of the creation process that once begun were unending and thus ever creating anew. So too is it with you.

8.6   Each expression of God's love, being of God, continued to express love through expression of its nature, which was of God. What happened in the case of human beings, was a disconnect from your own true nature, which in turn caused a disconnect in your ability to express love, which in turn caused a disconnect in your ability to know God, because you did not know your Self.

8.7   The expression of your true nature should never have been difficult, joyless, or fearful, but you cannot imagine what a creative undertaking the human being was! If you can imagine for a moment yourself as a being whose every thought became manifest, as perhaps you can envision from remembering your dreams in which anything can happen without any need for you to "do" anything, and then becoming a form where expressing yourself depended upon what you could "do" with the human body, you can imagine the learning process that ensued. If your reality had been like unto the reality you experience in dreams, can you not see that you would have to learn to breathe, to speak, to walk, as a baby learns to do these things, and that these things were loving acts within a loving universe, a love-filled learning process. A learning process that was as known to you and chosen by you as it was by God, because you and God are one.

8.8   You might ask how, if what I'm saying is true, could God disconnect from Himself? What God could not disconnect from was the true nature of the being of God, which is love. What God could not disconnect from was the true nature of creation, which is love. What God, in effect had to do, what *you* in effect had to do, in order to live in a nature inconsistent with what God could not disconnect from, was disconnect from God. Since God was the center of your being, it was impossible to disconnect your heart and still live. What could be disconnected was your will, or in other words, your mind. Just as it is your nature to breathe oxygen, and not breathing oxygen is inconsistent with your nature, fearfulness is inconsistent with God. Judgment is inconsistent with God. Bondage or lack of freedom is inconsistent with God.

8.9   God always knew what your mind chose to rebel against: that creation is perfect. Your mind, being of God, was constrained by the learning limits of the body and chose to rebel against the learning that was needed in order to come into the time of fullness of a being able to express itself in form, never realizing that this just delayed the learning that had to occur to release you from the limits you struggled against. The constant striving to be more and more, faster and faster — each being's yearning, passionate, excessive drive to fulfill its purpose, like a drive to explore the ocean before knowing how to swim or a drive to explore new lands while still believing the Earth to be flat, God saw and knew to be consistent with the nature of man, even while the fear and struggle that this impatience with the process of creation generated was inconsistent with God.

8.10   Thus, what could God then do? What does creation do with a storm arising on the horizon, growing out of atmospheric conditions perfect to generate its violence? What do you who are parents do with a child who is too impatient, too bright, too eager, to learn slowly and to mature gracefully? Do you withdraw your love? Never. Do you disinherit? Rarely. What you do is realize the impossibility of imposing your will and, because of this impossibility, you realize that you must let go. Thus your decision was also God's decision.

8.11   In following in the way of God's original intent, you rebelled against God's original design, the design that is the pattern of creation.   Your rebellion was not with God, although you came to see it as such. Your rebellion was not *allowed*, it was mutually *chosen*. Just as, as a parent, you come to see that you cannot fight a child's nature, no matter how different it might be from your own; just as in extreme cases you see that you cannot stop your child from perilous behavior save by taking away his freedom through the most extreme of measures; this is what happened between you and God.

8.12   To take away your freedom in order to protect you, even from yourself, would not have been an act of love. To take away *your* freedom would be to take away God's own freedom, the freedom of creation. Your rebellion against the constraints of your nature in form became part of the pattern of creation because it was the created's response. It was *your* response, and since God is both the Creator and the Created, it was God's response as well.

8.13   As you begin to live as both the Created and the Creator, you expand and enrich God. What other purpose would God ever have had for wanting to express the Love that is Himself in form, if it were not for the expansion and enrichment it would add to His being? What purpose is behind your own desire to do thus?

8.14   It was only the ego that made this desire seem to be for anything other than the purpose of expansion and enrichment of your being. If it is only in sharing who you are, through expression of who you are, that you come to know who you are, then this is true of God as well. God could not be the only being in all of creation who remains static and unchanging! How could this possibly be said of one whose name and identity is synonymous with creation? You like to think that God knows everything, and God surely knows everything that *is*. But consciousness of what *is*, the Christ-consciousness that allows you to be in communion with God, is not a static state. While consciousness of the truth is never-changing, consciousness of the truth is also ever-expanding.

8.15 Does one know love in one burst of knowing and never know more of love? Does one *grasp* beauty and thereafter remain ever unstirred by it? Is not the very essence of consciousness itself this ability to come to know continuously? To be aware constantly of what *is,* is to continuously come to know and yet to never not know.

8.16 You think of a state of knowing as a state in which there is nothing you do not know about something. This is why you study subjects — so that you can come to this completion and enjoy this certainty and pride that at least you know all there is to know about this one thing. This was the ego's answer to being a learning being — choosing something to learn that it could master. This desire to be done with learning, which is a true desire, is consistent with your true nature and your purpose here. To learn everything there is to know about even one subject and to call that learning complete, however, is an error. If you re-think this definition you will see that even in regard to the learning of one subject it is not the truth. The only instance in which this is the truth is in regard to learning who you are.

8.17 Learning, dear brothers and sisters, does come to an end, and that end is fast approaching. Coming to know through learning will be of the past as soon as Christ-consciousness is sustainable and you begin to come to know through constant revelation of what *is*. True learning has had only one purpose...the purpose of returning you to awareness of your true identity. Be done with learning now as you accept who you truly are.

chapter 9

Beyond Learning

9.1   Learning is not meant to last. This is why even this *course work* comes to an end. It comes to an end here and now as we move past *study* and *learning* to observation, vision, and revelation.

9.2   All groups who *study* this *course work* must also eventually come to an end. For this *end* to learning is the goal toward which we now work.

9.3   You have realized that all of your learning and studying has taken you as far as you can go. You complete your study of Christianity and go on to study Buddhism. You complete your study of Buddhism and go on to study any number of other religions, philosophies, sciences. You read books that are channeled, books that tell of personal experiences, books that promise ten steps to success. You go out in search of experiences of a mystical nature. You have tried drugs or hypnosis, meditation or work with energy. You have read and listened and been enthralled by those who have synthesized all of the great learning that has gone on so that they can tell you where it is that all these great teachings are leading. All of these learned works that speak the truth — from ancient times through current times — are learned works that have been worthy of your study. These learned works are the precursors that have shown the way to creating unity and relationship through unity and relationship.

9.4   But now the time is upon you to leave learned works behind in favor of observation, vision, and revelation. Now is the time to leave behind study for imagining, envisioning, and desire. Now is the time to move out of the time of becoming who you are to the time of being who you are.

9.5   You have felt this time coming. You have realized that your learning has reached an end point. The excitement of new learning is not lasting because it is not new. You have begun to see that all messages of the truth say the same thing but in different ways. There seems to be nothing new to be said, nothing to move you beyond this point that you have reached in your understanding of the truth. All the learning that you have done seems to leave you ready to change and able to change in certain ways that make life easier or more peaceful, but certainly not able to realize the transformation that your learning has seemed to promise.

9.6   Do not accept this lack of fulfillment of a promise that has surely been made! Rejoice that the new time is here and be ready to embrace it as it embraces you!

9.7   Realize that the self-centeredness of the final stage of your learning has been necessary. Only by centering your study upon yourself have you been made ready finally to be loosed of the bounds of the personal self. This time of concentration on the self is unheralded in history. It is what has been needed. Be grateful to all of the forerunners of the new who have been courageous enough to call you to examine yourself. Be grateful to yourself that you have had the courage to listen and to learn and to study what these forerunners of the new, these prophets of the new, have called you to learn. Be appreciative of every tool that has advanced your progress. But now be willing to leave them behind.

9.8   These have been the last of the intermediaries, these called to a wisdom beyond their personal capacity. Now these forerunners of the new, along with you, are called to step beyond what they have learned to what can only be revealed.

These are my beloved, along with you, and these next words an entreaty meant especially for them.

9.9   You who have provided a service cherished by God, and who have risen in the esteem of your brothers and sisters, be beacons now to the new. You who have gained so much through your learning and your study and your sharing of the same may find it difficult to leave it behind. A choice made by you to stay with learning rather than to move beyond it would be an understandable choice, but you are needed now. Needed to help establish the covenant of the new. Be not afraid, for the glory that has been yours will be as nothing to the glory that awaits you in the creation of the new. You will always be honored for what you have done. But do you want this to be forever the cause of your honor? Be willing to be the forerunners still, to join your brothers and sisters in this next phase of the journey, the journey out of the time of learning that will usher in the fullness of time.

chapter 10

Creating Anew

10.1   This course has led you through resigning as your own teacher, to becoming a true student, and to now leading you beyond the time of being a student to the realization of your accomplishment. You were once comfortable being your own teacher. You willingly gave up that role and became comfortable in the true role of learner. You are now asked to be willing to give up the role of learner and to believe that you will become comfortable and more in your new role as the accomplished.

10.2   This is hard for you to imagine because, as you consider your willingness to give up learning, you will meet resistance and realize, for perhaps the first time, that learning is what your entire life has been about. You cannot imagine how you will come to know anything new or be anything beyond that which you now are without learning. Your thoughts might stray to ideas about experiencing rather than studying and yet you will quickly see that you merely think of experience as learning through a different means than studying.

10.3   As you have advanced along your self-centered path of learning, you have come to see everything in your life as exactly what it has been: a means of learning. You have encountered problems and wondered what lessons they have come to teach you. You have encountered illness and wondered what learning the illness has come to bring you. You have learned anew from your past. Learned from your dreams. Learned from art and music. In all of these things you have viewed yourself as the learner. You may not have *studied* your problems, illness, your past, your dreams, or art and music as you *studied* the lessons that kept you focused on your Self, but you did, in a sense, study every aspect of your life for the lessons contained therein. So how, you might ask, do you now quit doing what you have so long done?

10.4   In keeping with your new self-centered focus on what life has had to teach you, you have also seen your relationships as teachers. It is here that you can begin to learn to let go of learning because it is here that learning has been least practiced through the means of studying.

10.5   Relationship happens in the present moment. Studying takes up residence within the student there to be mulled over, committed to memory, integrated into new behaviors. Relationship recognizes that love is the greatest teacher. Studying places the power of the teacher in a place other than that of love. Relationship happens as it happens. Studying is about future outcome. What happens in relationship has present moment meaning. What is studied has potential meaning.

10.6   The outcome of learning, or of what is studied, is the production of things and perceived meaning.

10.7   What we work toward now is to advance from learning and producing *things* and *perceived meaning*, to producing unity and relationship through unity and relationship.

10.8   The *learning* that was applied to anything other than the Self could not help but have an outcome that had to do with other than the Self. Means and end are one, cause and effect the same. Thus this applied learning produced things and perceived meaning.

10.9   The learning you have accomplished in regard to your Self could not help but have an outcome that had to do with your Self. Means and end are one, cause and effect the same. This accomplished learning produced unity and relationship through unity and relationship with the Self.

10.10   The first accomplishment of your learning about your Self was the return of unity and relationship to your mind and heart. This returned to you your ability to recognize, or identify your Self as other than a separate being, and led the way to your recognition of the state of union. From this recognition of unity and relationship the production of unity and relationship and true meaning will be revealed.

10.11   Learning has had to do with what is perceived. *No longer learning* has to do with what is revealed. Learning has had to do with what is unknown. *No longer learning* has to do with what *is* and can only be known through revelation. Learning has had to do with supplying a lack. *No longer learning* has to do with the realization that there is no lack. Learning was what was necessary in order to allow you to fulfill the desired experience of expressing the Self of love in form. *No longer learning* is the revelation that the time of accomplishment is upon you and the expression of the Self of love in form is what you are now ready to do. Learning was what was necessary in order to know who you are and how to express who you are. *No longer learning*, or being accomplished, is synonymous with knowing who you are and the ability to express who you are in truth.

10.12   Expression of the Self of love in form is not something that can be learned. It is something that can only be lived. This is the time of the fulfillment of the lesson of the birds of the air who neither sough nor reap but sing a song of gladness. Expression of the Self of love is the natural state of being of those who have moved beyond learning to creating through unity and relationship.

10.13   As I said earlier, some will not be willing to move out of the time of learning. Those who have learned what this course would teach but do not move beyond the state of learning will change the world. They will make the world a better place and see many of their students advance beyond what they can teach and to the state of leaving learning behind.

10.14   Those of you willing to leave learning behind will create the new. This will not happen through learning but through sharing. You can learn to change the world, but not how to create a new world. Does this not make sense? You can learn about who you were and who others were, but you cannot learn anymore who you are or who those are who have joined you in Christ-consciousness, for you have become who you are and move on from this starting point to creating who you are anew in unity and relationship. You can learn from the past but not from the future. When you build upon what you can learn you build upon the past and create not the future but an extension of the past. You who are called to leave learning behind are called to return to your union and relationship with God wherein you are creators along with God.

chapter 11

Christ-Consciousness

11.1   The future is yet to be created. This is why I stated at the onset of this treatise that this treatise would not be predictive. Many predictions of the future have been made, and many of them have been called prophecy. But the future is yet to be created.

11.2   The future depends on you who are willing to leave learning behind and who are willing to accept your new roles as creators of the new — creators of the future.

11.3   Can I teach you to do this? My dear brothers and sisters in Christ, as you once willingly resigned as your own teacher, I now willingly resign as your teacher. In unity there is no need for teachers or for learners. There is need only for the sustainability of Christ-consciousness in which we exist together as creators in unity and relationship.

11.4   Thus I will conclude this treatise with a prelude to the sharing that is our new means of communicating and creating, a sharing that replaces learning with what is beyond learning. I conclude this treatise by sharing that which will assist you in sustaining Christ-consciousness.

11.5   As I do so, I bid you to read these words in a new way. You are no longer a learner here and what I reveal to you must be regarded as the equal sharing of brothers and sisters in Christ, the sharing of fellow creators in unity and relationship. This is the beginning of our co-creation. Do not seek for me to impart knowledge to you in these concluding words. Absorb the following pages as a memory returned to your reunited heart and mind. No longer regard me as an authority to whom you turn but as an equal partner in the creation of the future through the sustainability of Christ-consciousness.

chapter 12

A Prelude to the Dialogues

12.1   Welcome, my new brothers and sisters in Christ, to the creation of the future through the sustainability of Christ-consciousness. Today we join together to birth the new.

12.2   From this time on, I will respond to you through direct communication or dialogue rather than through teaching. As with all new means of doing anything, this dialogue must have a starting point. This is it.

12.3   At this time, there is a gathering of pioneers of the new already in existence. They are beginning to see that they learn as one. They are beginning to see that their questions are the same. They are beginning to see that they share in means not confined to the physical senses.

12.4   This prelude will address them individually and collectively, and as you join with them in unity, you will realize that it also addresses you individually and as part of the collectivity of the whole. This dialogue will be ongoing, and this is your invitation to participate in this dialogue. No matter where you are, no matter what concerns you still hold within your heart, no matter what questions are emanating from your mind, they will be met with a response.

12.5   Two changes of enormous proportions are upon you. The first is the end of learning, the ramifications of which will only slowly occur to your mind and be surprising revelations there. The second is the beginning of sharing in unity, a change that your heart will gladly accept but that your mind, once again, will be continuously surprised to encounter.

12.6   Take delight in these surprises. Laugh and be joyous. You no longer have a need to figure things out. Surprises cannot be figured out! They are meant to be joyous gifts being constantly revealed. Gifts that need only be received and responded to.

12.7   Once these dialogues are sustainable without need of the written word, the written word will be less necessary. In the meantime, let me explain why these written words are not the acts of an intermediary and why they represent direct sharing.

12.8   The simple and complete explanation of the non-intermediary nature of this dialogue is that it exists in unity. It is given and received in unity. Intermediary steps were needed only for the separate state. All conditions that were intermediary in nature during the time of learning, are, during the time of sharing, naturally converted to direct experiences of sharing.

12.9   Thus, if you have been religious, abandon not your churches, for you will find within them now, direct experiences of sharing. If you have found guidance and comfort in the written word, abandon not the written word, for the written word will now elicit direct experiences of sharing. If you have enjoyed learning through gatherings of students, gather still, and experience sharing directly. If a time arrives when you no longer feel drawn to these modes of sharing, share anew in ever-wider configurations.

12.10   All you must remember now is that the time of learning is past. While you are still encountering concerns and questions, you will be prone to continue to think of yourself as a learning being. While these dialogues continue to address these same questions and concerns, you will be prone to think of them as teaching dialogues and to consider yourself still a student. Considering yourself thus is simply a condition of the old that you will need to be vigilant of. You will be again surprised to find what an enormous difference the release of this idea will make in your capacity to express who you are. As long as you continue to invite learning, you will continue to invite the *conditions* of learning. These are the conditions you have experienced throughout your lifetime and have expressed a willingness to leave behind. Only you can leave these conditions behind. The only way to do so is to, for a short while, be vigilant of your thought patterns so that you eradicate the idea of learning in separation and replace it with the idea of sharing in unity. Learning is a condition of the separated self, which is why it is no longer needed. You will not fully realize unity while you continue to hang on to this condition of the separation.

12.11 Another thing that you will want to be vigilant of, dear brothers and sisters, is the learned wisdom of the past. Let me give you an example that relates to the state of rebellion that was discussed within the text of this treatise.

12.12 This example arose from one of those already gathered who was questioning the state of contentment. She quoted a learned priest and scholar who spoke of how he knew, as soon as he was content within the life of the monastery, that it was time to once again move out into the world. What he was really saying was that he saw the dawning of his contentment as the sign that one period of learning was over and that it was time to move on to the next. During the time of learning, this statement was consistent with learned wisdom. During the new time of sharing, there is no "next phase" of learning for you to move on to. There is no reason for you not to exist in continual contentment. Continual contentment will not stunt your growth or prevent you from sharing or from expressing yourself anew.

12.13 Is this not a good example of the *learned wisdom* that needs to be left behind? But what of the questions its raises? Do you not respond to the idea of continual contentment with doubt? Not only doubt that it can be continual but with doubt that you would desire it to be? These questions relate to our earlier discussion of temptations of the human experience. Are you willing to leave them behind? Are you willing, for instance, to leave behind the idea that contentment cannot and *should* not last? That lasting contentment, like unto a lasting peace, would somehow stunt your growth? Can you see that your idea of growth was synonymous with your idea of learning? That you were always both awaiting and dreading your next learning challenge?

12.14 Why was this so? You eagerly awaited each learning challenge in the hopes that it would bring you to the state in which you now abide! You dreaded each learning challenge because you feared that it would not bring you to this state and that you would continue to need to learn and to perhaps suffer from the conditions of learning!

12.15 You have arrived! The long journey that brought you here is over. Grow not impatient or desirous of a return to journeying before you begin to experience the joy of sharing and the new challenges of creating the new! This will be joyous journeying and your challenges will be joyous challenges!

12.16 The state of rebellion was the effect of the cause of learned wisdom. It became part of the nature of the human experience by becoming so consistent within man that it came to be integral to your nature through the passing down of the learned wisdom of the human experience. Have you not always been told and seen examples of man pushing against his limits? Has not this pushing against limits been called progress? Have not even the most devastating misuses of power attained through this rebellion been seen retrospectively as having advanced the cause of man's evolution and society's knowledge?

12.17   This is just a beginning point of your ability to see what learned wisdom has wrought. This is a necessary end point of your review of your experience here so that you do not continue to advance learned wisdom. Learned wisdom will tell you to work hard. Learned wisdom will tell you that the strong survive, the mighty prevail, the weak shall perish. I attempted to dislodge much of this learned wisdom during my time on Earth and man is still puzzling over the meaning of my words. The time for puzzlement is over. Pass on no more of the prevailing learned wisdom. I told you once we would create a new language and so we shall! We are creators of the new and we must start somewhere. Why not here?

12.18   Think and speak no more of the suffering of the past. Spread the joyous news! Tell only joyous stories. Advance the idea of joyous challenges that allow for all the creativity you have put into challenges of the past but without the struggle. Let not the idea of struggle take hold in the new. Let not the idea of fear take hold in the new. Let not the idea of judgment take hold in the new. Announce far and wide freedom from the old ideas, the learned wisdom of old. What could be more invigorating, more challenging, more stimulating to your enrichment, than throwing out the old and beginning again? And doing so without effort, without struggle. What could be more looked forward to than the chance to create the new through sharing in unity and relationship with your brothers and sisters in Christ?

12.19   I know you still have questions, dear brothers and sisters. I know that you will experience times of not knowing how to proceed. I know that you will occasionally have setbacks and choose the conditions of learning instead of sharing in unity in order to realize some bit of knowledge that you feel is necessary before you can go on. But I ask you to try

257

to remember to turn to the new rather than the old each time you think you are experiencing uncertainty or lack.

12.20　The only thing that is going to hold you back from your ability to sustain Christ-consciousness is doubt about yourself. You must constantly remember that doubt about yourself is fear, and reject the instinct, so engrained into your singular consciousness, to let doubt of yourself take hold of you. Even though you are abiding now in the state of Christ-consciousness, the *pattern* of the old thoughts will continue until they are replaced by a new pattern. That self-doubt arises in your thought patterns will not mean that you have cause for self-doubt. You have no cause for self-doubt because you have no cause for fear. To dwell in fear will end your ability to dwell within the love that is Christ-consciousness.　As there is no longer any cause for self-doubt there are no *reasons* for self-doubt.　Do not examine yourself for reasons for self-doubt when it arises.　The self-centeredness of the final stage of learning is over.

12.21　Your "centeredness" must now be focused on sharing in unity and relationship, and creating anew in unity and relationship.　Along with the creation of a new language, another imperative creation with which to begin our new work is that of new patterns.　The patterns of old were patterns designed for the optimal benefit of learning. These patterns were created by the one mind and heart that you share in unity with God.　The new patterns of sharing in unity and relationship, and creating unity and relationship, are only now being created by the one mind and heart that you share in unity with God.　You will be the co-creator of the new pattern of consciousness that is sharing in unity and relationship, as you were once the co-creator of the pattern of consciousness that was learning.

12.22　Again let me remind you that we are speaking of the new. There has always been a state of consciousness that we are here calling Christ-consciousness. There has never been a sustained Christ-consciousness in form. The Christ-consciousness that has always existed, a consciousness of what *is*, is an all-inclusive consciousness, the consciousness of the embrace. It is not a learned state, as was the singular consciousness of the human form. It is your innate consciousness, a consciousness far too vast to be learned but one easily shared by all.

12.23 In other words, you, as a being of singular consciousness, could learn the thought patterns of a singular consciousness because it was a finite consciousness, a consciousness with limits. You, as a being joined in Christ-consciousness, must share this consciousness *in order* to know it. It cannot be grasped by the singular consciousness. You could think of this as the integration into the thought processes of the singular brain that which would cause brain *damage*, because it would cause an overload of information. The singular consciousness would act like a computer with a full drive and reject the information or be overcome by it if such were possible. Such is not possible, because Christ-consciousness is not available to the separated self. Christ-consciousness is the consciousness of unity for unity is what *is*.

12.24 Thus you now exist within a shared conscious-ness. The pattern of a shared consciousness is one of sharing in unity and relationship. There is no pattern within it for learning (which is individual), for individual gain, or for individual accomplishment.

12.25 But realize, those of you who would mourn this as a loss, that you have already achieved all that was possible to achieve as an individual. The purpose of individual learning was the return of unity! Pause a moment here, and celebrate this feat of the personal self! The personal self, through the self-centeredness of the final stages of learning, has achieved the ultimate achievement possible! Let yourself be grateful for the learning you have achieved. Celebrate this graduation, this anointing, this passage. And leave it behind. Realize that it has made you new. Rejoice and be glad and turn your attention to the new. Attend to the dawning of the consciousness of unity. Realize that it is a truly *new* state, a state that cannot be learned, a state the awareness of which can only be revealed to you through unity and relationship.

12.26 Realize this without fear, for I am with you. This is akin to being stranded in a foreign land with none of the ways you learned to adapt in the past being of service to you. That is how new this is, and more. But the difference is that you are not alone and that you are not in a foreign land but returned to your home of origin. What you cannot learn you can remember. What you cannot learn will simply be known through sharing.

12.27 It is the *way* in which you will come to remember and share in unity that concerns you now and what we are speaking of when we talk of patterns. There was a pattern to the process of learning that was shared by all learners and inherent to your nature as learning beings. The means were different for each, but the pattern was the same. There was an overall design that ensured optimal learning and that design was known to you in the pattern of that design, a pattern that was part of the pattern of your thoughts, even after the ego came to rule your thought system. Without this pattern, the ego could have succeeded in becoming the ruler of the personal self. Part of this design and pattern was the freedom of free will.

12.28 Free will continues in the pattern of Christ-consciousness. Love continues. The individual or singular consciousness that was appropriate to the time of learning does not continue. The new pattern is one of creation in relationship and unity rather than learning. What this means will be revealed to you and shared by all who abide within

Christ-consciousness because you abide in a consciousness of unity through your choice.

12.29   You do not have to choose to share because you cannot *not* share.   You do not have to continually choose unity, because you have already chosen unity and abide there.   You do, however, have to refrain from choosing separation.   You do have to refrain from choosing learning and the conditions of learning.

12.30   What will help you to remain doubt-free, fear-free, and continually able to sustain Christ-consciousness, is coming to know the new design and the new patterns that reveal the design.   This new design and the new patterns that will be helpful to you in its sustainability is what must be created through our sharing in unity and be communicated through our continuing dialogues with one another.

12.31   This is a prelude to but one form of these dialogues. Sharing in unity is automatic.   It is the nature of Christ-consciousness.   Once you have adapted to this nature you will realize that what is communicated through our dialogues and those you share with your brothers and sisters, is simply communication of what already *is*.   This will help you to adapt to the revelations that replace learning.   This will help you to adapt to the truth of a sharing you will have received even before it is communicated through the means you are accustomed to.   It will help us together to establish the new patterns by which you, and those who come after you, will more fully come to awareness of all they have inherited and all it is within their power to create.

12.32   I do not have the answers that would continue to make of me a teacher and you a student.   The answers to the elevation of the personal self and the living of Christ-consciousness in form are yet to be revealed and shared.   This is the time that is before us, the time of creation of the future, the time of the creation of a future not based upon the past.

12.33 This time is before *us*. Because you are a being still existing in form, you still exist in the realm of time and space. Yet time and space no longer separate us, and the creation of the design or pattern that reveals our lack of separation is part of the creation that is before *us*. It will be mutually decided through the coming revelations and our responses to the revelations of the new.

12.34 Creation of the new has begun. We are an interactive part of this creative act of a loving Creator. Creation is a dialogue. Creation — which is God and us in unity, will respond to our responses, will respond to what we envision, imagine, and desire. Creation of the new could not begin without you. Your willingness for the new, a willingness that included the leaving behind of the old, a willingness that included the leaving behind of fear and judgment and a separate will, was necessary to begin creation of the new. Your former willingness to accept the old but kept creation's power harnessed to the old. Does this not make perfect sense when you realize that creation, like God, is not "other than" who you are? How could creation proceed on to the new without you?

12.35 What will the future hold? It is up to us, dear brothers and sisters. It is up to us acting as one body, one mind, one heart. It is up to us creating as one body, one mind, one heart. Because it is the new future of a new form joined in unity and relationship, the only guarantees that are known to us is that it will be a future of love, a future without fear, a future with unlimited freedom. For what more could we ask? And what more could be asked of us?

12.36 Make no mistake that what is asked of us is everything. What is asked is our total willingness to abandon the old, our total willingness to embrace the new. But also make no mistake

that what is given to us is everything. All the power of creation
is released onto us. Let us begin.

The Treatises of A Course of Love were given by the voice of Jesus and expressed in writing by Mari Perron.

Course of Love Publications is dedicated to the materials, individuals, and relationships associated with the Course of Love.

The way of the heart described in this book is often shared in group and private settings. If you would like to share information about your group, acquire assistance in starting a group, or arrange a presentation, please contact:

Course of Love Publications
432 Rehnberg Place
W. St. Paul, Minnesota 55118
acol@thedialogues.com

The books of the Course of Love series are available toll free at 1-800-901-3480, at bookstores by special order, from on-line retailers, or through the following websites:

www.acourseoflove.com
and www.ItascaBooks.com